HOW TO WRITE
AND DELIVER

Effective
Speeches

4th Edition

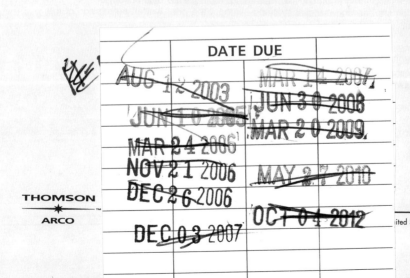

THOMSON
ARCO

11/02   12.95

THOMSON
———✴———™
ARCO

Dedication

To my mother who taught me the importance of being oneself and believing in oneself, and to my students and clients who have demonstrated the truth of my mother's teachings.

Contents

Chapter One: Getting Started   1
    Speech Anxiety   2
    Types Of Delivery   4
    Purpose of Speech   5
        General Purposes   6
        Specific Purposes   7
    Logos, Ethos, And Pathos   8
    Using An Outline   9
    Summary   11

Chapter Two: Getting Organized   13
    The Three Parts of a Speech   14
        The Introduction   14
        The Body   18
        The Conclusion   23
    Transitions   25
    Summary   27

Chapter Three: Using Evidence   29
    Quotations   30
    Statistics   32
    Narration   33
    Definitions   36
    Summary   37

Chapter Four: Research and Documentation   39
   Interviews   40
   Surveys   42
   Computer Searches   42
   Library Reference Materials   43
   Periodicals—Newspapers, Magazines, And Journals   45
   Electronic Media   46
   Documenting Your Research   47
      APA Style for Recording a Book   47
   Summary   53

Chapter Five: Using Language   55
   Style   56
      Denotative and Connotative Meanings   56
      Figurative Language   57
   Cultural Considerations   58
      Nonsexist Language   58
      Dialect   62
   Common Errors In Language   63
      Pointless Words and Phrases   63
      Frequently Misused Words   63
   Summary   67

Chapter Six: Delivering Your Speech   69
   Nonverbal Delivery   70
      Eye Contact   70
      Posture and Stance   71
      Gestures and Movement   72
      Facial Expression   73
      Dress   73
   Verbal Delivery   74
      Volume   74
      Rate   75

Pitch   75

Nonfluencies   76

Pronunciation and Enunciation   77

External Factors   79

Summary   80

Chapter Seven: Using Visual Aids   81

Functions Of Visual Aids   81

Three-Dimensional Aids   83

Posters   83

Flip Charts And Boards   84

Overhead Transparencies   85

Photographs And Slides   86

Videotape   87

Handouts   88

Summary   89

Chapter Eight: Listening, Evaluating, and Perfecting   91

Listening   91

Evaluation   93

Summary   101

Preface

If the thought of giving a speech causes you to panic—relax. Everyone feels some degree of trepidation when asked to speak in front of an audience. Moreover, anyone who wants to become more comfortable communicating can improve his or her abilities. By following the logical, pragmatic, and succinct speechmaking steps in this book, you *will* become a more effective communicator.

How to Write and Deliver an Effective Speech is based on the experiences of thousands of individuals who conquered their anxieties about speaking in front of others. This book demystifies the art of public speaking by examining three manageable yet essential aspects of presentations. First, *How to Write and Deliver an Effective Speech* negates irrational fears about speaking by presenting practical tips that will replace your phobia with your desire to improve your speaking abilities. Second, you will discover the essential yet easy-to-follow steps involved in creating a meaningful message that the audience will not forget. Third, you will learn the elements of delivery that result in a dynamic presentation. By eliminating your feats, perfecting *what* you say and *how* you say it, *How to Write and Deliver an Effective Speech* will help you to change the way you view public speaking. So forget about pressing the panic button—read on, and become the great speaker you have always wanted to be.

Chapter One

Getting Started

When asked about their number one fear in life, most people state that public speaking is the dreaded culprit. However, when asked about one of the most important skills in life, people also mention public speaking. What appears to be an unusual dichotomy is actually quite understandable. Research has demonstrated that good presentation skills can result in more success in school, hiring and promotions in the workplace, a more positive image, and improved self-confidence and esteem. In other words, the more skillful we are at getting our ideas across, the better results we'll have in life. And yet, even though we understand this at a cognitive level, most of us still feel butterflies in our stomachs or fall into that unsettling, anxious state when asked to speak before others.

People generally state that their anxieties about speaking are caused by a fear that they will make a mistake, forget what to say, or look nervous. In essence, although most people recognize the positive significance of effective speaking skills, they lack the confidence and skills to perform in front of an audience.

By providing concepts, tips, and guidelines, this book will give you the essential pragmatic information you need to create a positive attitude and improve your speechmaking skills. Through succinct, step-by-step instruction, this book will make writing and delivering a speech, in addition to speaking more informally in front of others, a joy instead of a chore.

This first chapter will examine the first step in the process of speechmaking. It looks at ways to handle speech anxiety; types of speech delivery; purposes for writing speeches; wisdom and practicality for contemporary times from the fourth-century B.C. Greek philosopher, Aristotle; and the importance of using outlines. So, let's get started and take a look at the frequently experienced, yet easily disregarded, speech anxiety.

SPEECH ANXIETY

At one time or another, everyone has experienced the rapidly pounding heart, pulsing blood, sweaty palms, blushing, or shortness of breath associated with speaking in front of a group. Some people are so frightened that they walk away from a potentially advantageous situation. If you've ever rejected a chance to speak or experienced some of the previously mentioned symptoms, then consider carefully the following list of truths and incorporate them into your knowledge of public speaking.

First, a speaker's state of nervousness is not that obvious; your audience will probably never be aware of your fear. Beginning speakers inevitably report how terrified they were during their first speeches only to find out that nobody in the audience knew they were afraid. Many famous celebrities, politicians, and CEOs of major corporations experience an increased pulse rate and sweaty palms before speaking, but their audience just can't tell. Just as an athlete experiences a rush of adrenaline before a sporting event, so do performers and speakers before going in front of their audience.

The important thing is to channel this excitement and alertness into enthusiasm and passion for your subject matter. A certain degree of trepidation leads to an increased intensity, quicker thought, and a more stimulating delivery instead of an apathetic, dull, and canned presentation. Few people are born with the ability to deliver a stimulating and effective speech, but you can learn to be a spontaneous speaker and channel your fears into energy, animation, and persuasiveness.

Second, it's of utmost importance to realize that most audiences are approving and accepting. They want to see you do well and succeed so that they will benefit in some way from your talk. As a speaker, you need to have a positive view of your audience by assuming that you will be accepted and do well rather than being caught up in false notions that your audience is there to embarrass and criticize.

Third, you need to humanize yourself just by being yourself. It doesn't work to pretend to be someone you're not. Unless you're a great actor, pretentions, affectations, and false personas don't work when giving a speech. The most successful speeches are given by people who reach their audience, who establish rapport by setting a personal tone and connecting with the audience. A down-to-earth delivery can make each person in the audience feel as though you are speaking to him or her individually. This is exactly the result you want.

Fourth, stop thinking about yourself and how you will do, and concentrate on your audience and your subject matter. Just as in interpersonal relationships, when you spend too much time thinking about how you're coming across, you miss out on the feedback you are receiving from others. Relax, act and feel confident, and focus on your objectives for speaking.

Fifth, begin your talk with a pause and short sentences. It's best to start slowly, gaining the attention and approval of your audience with an effective and clearly stated introduction, rather than to lose your listeners at the start of your speech with a rapid beginning. A pause and short sentences at the start of your talk will assist audiences in remembering where you're headed instead of wondering what they missed or where you're going. It's also never a good idea to qualify your speech with statements such as, "I'm really not an expert in this area," or "I'm really scared to death up here." Take control and recognize that you're in front of the group for a reason, be proud of the work you've put into your written material, and realize that audiences want a speaker who will take command and lead them to a higher cognitive or emotional level.

Last, preparation and practice are the only ways to improve your skills. Take every opportunity to speak in front of others. Just as a musician or an athlete improves with consistent practice, so will you. When you are requested to give a formal talk, spend time preparing your talk, use an outline during your presentation, and practice in front of a mirror. Many speakers audiotape or videotape their rehearsals. This is an excellent way to discover things about your delivery that you particularly like or might want to change. A videotape can reinforce an effective use of gestures or help you identify a lack of organization. It's interesting to note that most people are their own worst critics, and this is particularly true in speech self-evaluation. Research has demonstrated that when viewing their own prerecorded presentation, speakers are pleasantly surprised to see how well they performed. The bottom line is that spending time preparing and practicing your speech will improve your skills.

By incorporating these beginning steps into your speechmaking process, you'll find that your speech anxiety decreases as your interest and enthusiasm for speaking increase.

Tips to Eliminate Speech Anxiety

1. Realize that your audience will probably not recognize your fear.

2. Recognize that audiences are approving and accepting. They want you to succeed.

3. Humanize your delivery. Don't try to be someone you're not.

4. Concentrate on your subject matter and your audience, not yourself.

---

5. Take a few breaths before you begin, pause, and go slowly with short sentences in your introduction.

6. Prepare and practice. You should spend 60 percent of your time preparing your speech, then spend the rest of the time practicing in front of others, a mirror, or a recorder.

TYPES OF DELIVERY

The most common form of oral communication is conversation—the kind you have every day at school or work and in social situations. Normally your conversations are spontaneous, relaxed, and delivered without any preparation or practice. Public speaking, however, is a structured form of oral communication that consists of an individual speaking to an audience in one of four styles of delivery:

- Extemporaneous
- Impromptu
- Memorized
- Manuscript

Extemporaneous speaking begins with research, and then involves organizing your information and writing your text. Usually a speaker creates an outline composed of either complete sentences or phrases, then uses this outline during the actual speech. In extemporaneous speaking, you deliver an organized and documented speech that appears to be spontaneous even though you've had lots of time to prepare and practice. Because an outline of main points and supporting evidence is used in an extemporaneous speech, the speaker has the latitude to vary spoken words each time delivering the speech. This freedom in the choice of words adds to the spontaneity of the delivery.

Impromptu speaking sounds the most natural of all the styles of delivery because it is just that—the type of public speaking that is most clearly associated with conversation. Impromptu speaking occurs when you deliver a message based on information you have in your head. There is no time for preparation or practice, and therefore no time to create written materials to use during your speech. Although impromptu speaking occurs truly on the spur of the moment, to be effective it must be organized, coherent, and presented clearly and concisely. Many professional speakers and speech associations state that impromptu speaking improves as a speaker becomes more proficient in the other styles of delivery.

A *memorized* delivery is one that the speaker presents word for word as written by the speaker or a speech writer. The speaker doesn't use any written materials during the speech, because of having committed each word to memory. Actors, of course, are quite adept at delivering a scripted oration without any written document. Two important keys to memorized speeches are to make sure that you don't mix up words or even paragraphs, and to remain spontaneous. Most actors and famous speakers agree that the more practice in memorizing and delivering a memorized speech, the better the speech is.

Manuscript delivery occurs when every word is written out and spoken verbatim with the use of a written document. A manuscript speech is particularly effective when a crisis situation may depend on specific words being spoken. Many politicians and newscasters employ a manuscript delivery. Some of these speeches may even include parenthesized instructions in the written text as to where to look, point, or pause. Former President Ronald Reagan's speech writers were known for writing specific instructions in the president's speeches. Most newscasters use teleprompters that display information word for word during broadcasts. In contemporary society, when a president's words may be translated into hundreds of languages, or when a newscaster's report of a traumatic event may be viewed by millions of people, specific language expressed in a manuscript delivery is the only alternative for exactness in translation.

Although there are many differences between these four styles of delivery, they all have one important thing in common: Each style involves organized, clear, and succinct information, delivered with as much spontaneity as possible.

PURPOSE OF SPEECH

Whether you use an extemporaneous, impromptu, memorized, or manuscript style of delivery, you must have a purpose for speaking to others. Without a purpose, you could ramble on and on, unclear as to where you're headed and how you want your audience to respond. To assist you in defining your purpose, you need to take a good look at your audience by doing an *audience analysis*. An audience analysis is simply a description of your audience according to demographics. Because you would use different examples, language, and concepts when talking to diverse groups such as a third-grade class or a group of small-business owners, it's important to know exactly who you're speaking to. By adapting your speech to your audiences, you'll gain acceptance and understanding from them. So, ask yourself the following questions about your audiences:

- How old are they?
- Are they only men, only women, or both groups?
- At what educational and cultural level are they?

- What political and religious backgrounds do they represent?
- What is their ethnic composition?
- Do they speak a particular jargon?
- What do they know about your subject?
- What do they expect from your speech?
- How long will you be speaking to these groups?

Eventually you will get to the point where you automatically think about these questions, using the answers to assist you in writing your speech and reaching your audience. Kenneth Burke, a noted scholar and author of *Rhetoric of Motives,* noted the importance of knowing one's audience when he stated, "You persuade a man only insofar as you can talk his language by speech, gestures, tonality, order, image, attitude, idea, identifying your ways with his." Thus, it's best to know who you're trying to reach.

Having carefully considered who your audience is, you need to decide what response you want it to have. It is the speaker's responsibility to define the objective of the speech clearly. A clear and succinct purpose will lay the foundation for your talk, directing your audience to a specific result. And, as you know, you measure the ultimate success of your speech by what your audience receives.

General Purposes

The three general purposes in speaking are to inform, to persuade, and to entertain. By choosing a *primary general purpose,* you will become more specific about the response you want from your audience. Let's take a closer look at each general purpose.

When you *inform,* you are taking an objective position about a subject. You will present your talk as a teacher does, without bias, covering all sides of any position. As a result of a speech to inform, your audience will become more knowledgeable about a particular topic.

On the other hand, in a speech to *persuade,* you are trying to modify the thinking of the audience by getting them to agree with your subjective viewpoint. Persuasion has three subcategories, and all are motivational in nature. In a persuasive speech to *convince,* you want people to agree intellectually with your position. Lawyers spend a great deal of their time convincing judges and juries to accept their positions. In a persuasive speech to *actuate,* you want your audiences to take some physical action based on their conviction. Perhaps you will take up a collection after your speech or ask audiences to sign a petition. Advertising account executives work to actuate their clients to buy space or time in the media. In a persuasive speech to *inspire,* you give your audience hope or an emotional boost, uplifting their spirit. Ministers, rabbis, and other members of the clergy inspire their congregations with sermons.

In a speech to *entertain,* your primary goal is to keep the audience amused and interested. Comedians rely on stories, anecdotes, and particularly humor to keep an audience entertained.

Although you choose only one primary general purpose, you may also actually have one or even two secondary purposes. Even though a teacher may have a general purpose to inform, she may also have a secondary purpose to entertain, because humor adds a great deal to the effectiveness of learning. A problem would occur, however, if students were laughing at the expense of learning something. The bottom line is just to make sure that you are achieving your primary general purpose.

Specific Purposes

Once you know your general purpose, you need to combine it with the topic or subject of your speech to create a *specific purpose*. A specific purpose is what you want your audience to know, think, believe, or act on. Some examples of specific purposes include the following:

- To inform my audience about the most important person in my life
- To inform my audience about the three steps involved in making kites
- To entertain my audience with stories about my blind date
- To persuade my audience to vote for Dana for class president
- To persuade my audience that high-fat foods are bad for their health

Notice that the preceding examples combine a general purpose with a limited topic. If your topic is too broad, such as the history of sports, you'll have trouble covering all the material in a couple of days. If your topic is too general, it will also lack the details that make speeches fascinating and informative. A speaker can cover approximately three main points in about eight minutes, so think about narrowing your material to fit your time limit.

Note that your specific purpose will always include the word *audience* as a reminder to consider the receivers of your message. This is important because the ultimate test of the effectiveness of your talk is the response of that most important group, your audience.

After you've spent some time identifying a specific purpose, ask yourself the following three questions:

- Is there enough research available about my topic?
- Will my material fit the time limit?
- Am I really interested enough in this topic to spend the time involved?

If your answers to these questions are affirmative, then you've moved in the right direction toward getting the results you want from your audience.

LOGOS, ETHOS, AND PATHOS

In fourth-century B.C., Aristotle, a Greek philosopher and scholar, wrote a book entitled *Rhetoric,* which has withstood the test of time and scrutiny. Aristotle's ideas were so profound that they are as important today as they were in ancient Greek civilization. In *Rhetoric,* Aristotle stated that a speaker has philosophic responsibilities to his audience and that by incorporating three Greek concepts into the speechmaking process, a speaker can fulfill these responsibilities. The three concepts are logos, ethos, and pathos.

Logos refers to the logical structure of a speech. Logos is the reason or rational thought that the speaker uses to present the truth, real or apparent. When you use evidence and reasoning in your arguments, you are using logos. When you state, "There's a great deal of theft on our campus," and then support your statement with statistics and facts, you are incorporating logos into your presentation. A modern English derivative of logos is *logic,* which is reasoning.

Ethos is another important concept in speechmaking. This refers to the image or credibility the speaker conveys to the audience. A speaker with ethos is knowledgeable about his topic, prepared, sincere, believable, relaxed, and concerned about the audience. A modern derivative of this Greek term is *ethics.* A speaker with ethics earns the audience's trust.

Pathos is the emotion that speakers can evoke in their audiences. It's the sympathy, pity, infuriation, or disgust the audience feels as a result of a speech. The term pathos is still used in English today.

The important point to remember about Aristotle's wisdom is that a truly effective speaker incorporates reasoning, ethics, and emotion into the speechmaking process.

USING AN OUTLINE

An important written tool in speechmaking is an outline. An outline is basically a record of what you want to say in your speech. As a written abridgment of your talk, it divides your information into categorized data from broad to specific. So, rather than relying on a speech written out verbatim, you can glance at a summary composed of short sentences or phrases and know what to say. And because you won't be glued to a text, you'll spend more time relating to your audience spontaneously.

An outline is organized with main points designated by roman numerals, representing the major ideas. Subpoints are subordinate to main points, and as such, provide elaboration. Subpoints are identified by capital letters. Even more specific details in an outline are labeled, respectively, with Arabic numbers and then lowercase letters.

Examine the following outlining format:

Outlining Format

I. Main point
   A. Subpoint
      1. Even more specific material
      2. Even more specific material
   B. Subpoint
      1. More detailed information
      2. More detailed information
         a) Even more specific material
         b) Even more specific material

Notice how indentation occurs as your information moves from the broadest main points to the most specific subpoints. Now examine the first main point of a speech given to a group of students majoring in agricultural studies. The specific purpose of this speech is to persuade the audience that factory farming of veal at Slick Farm should be outlawed. The first main point illustrates inhumane practices in producing veal, whereas the second main point addresses the effect of that treatment. Look at the outline that was used for the first main point:

Factory Farming at Slick Farm

I. Slick Farm's factory farming of veal, raising animals in intense confinement, is inhumane.

   A. The life of a milk-fed veal calf is one of deprivation of exercise and light.

      1. From birth until slaughter, male calves spend their lives chained in a crate 22 inches by 58 inches.

         a) Calves cannot turn, groom, or lie down in a natural position.

         b) Calves are allowed no exercise.

      2. Calves are kept in total darkness.

         a) Lack of sunlight has a direct effect on calves' emotional and physical states.

         b) Former Slick Farm's employee, Irene Kilberger, recalls the panic and cries of calves.

   B. The diet of calves is cruel.

      1. Veal calves are denied all food and water.

         a) To quench their thirst, calves are given an unlimited supply of milk.

         b) An unnatural diet causes quick weight gain.

      2. To curb disease and achieve the most salable meat, veal calves are fed an overabundance of drugs.

         a) To create a light-colored meat, calves receive no iron.

         b) To fight infectious disease and promote growth, calves are given megadoses of antibiotics and hormones.

Although the actual spoken speech about factory farming was more elaborate and complex, the preceding extraction from the sentence outline demonstrates the form your outlines need to take. Just remember that outlines are aids to help you remember your information and stay spontaneous. Outlines are not your speech. As you become more adept at writing your own speech outlines, it will also become easier to take notes in lectures and recognize the main points in other peoples' speeches.

So, practice outlining and move one step closer to becoming a more effective speaker.

SUMMARY

This chapter discussed speech anxiety and how to rid yourself of this dreaded culprit; the four styles of speech delivery; three general purposes for giving speeches; how to write a specific purpose; the meaning and importance of the Greek terms *logos, ethos,* and *pathos;* and the essentials of outlining.

Now you're ready to move on to the next step in the process of preparing a speech—organizing your material.

Chapter Two

Getting Organized

It was an early Saturday morning. The audience eagerly awaited the speaker, who began:

> It's about time that we did something about pollution. Everyone is talking about it. I've spoken with hundreds of people who feel just like I do. Haven't you? In fact, I read something in the paper about pollution the other day. Did you? Sometimes I can see the smog. Can you? It's really something, isn't it?

Have you ever attended a speech where someone rambled on and on, and you wondered why you wasted a Saturday morning to hear someone who basically said nothing? Or have you ever been in a conversation and started thinking, "Where is he headed?" Perhaps during a lengthy lecture, you've thought, "Get to the point already!" Well if you have, you're not alone. Many speakers suffer from a lack of organization. Organization is the arrangement of interdependent ideas into a unified and cohesive message, and as such, it is extremely important in public speaking.

There are several reasons that a well-organized speech is an effective speech. First, research shows that a well-organized speech enhances a speaker's credibility or ethos by demonstrating clear thinking. Second, studies indicate that an effectively organized speech increases both comprehension and retention. Because you want your audience to trust you as a speaker and to understand and remember what you say, it makes perfect sense to spend the necessary time to organize your talk.

Now that you are aware of the need to write and deliver a well-organized speech, where do you begin? The best place to start is by examining the three parts of a speech and then looking at efficient ways to connect these parts. Therefore, this chapter covers important writing strategies for the introduction, body, and conclusion of your speech. You will also investigate clear and cohesive patterns for organizing the main points of your talk. Finally, this chapter discusses signposts—the words, phrases, or sentences that connect the three parts of your speech.

THE THREE PARTS OF A SPEECH

An effective speech should be divided into three basic units:

- Introduction
- Body
- Conclusion

Because the introduction is first, it must gain the interest and attention of your audience as well as provide the specific purpose or objective of your speech. The body consists of your main points and supporting material, and as such, is the place where you discuss your message in depth. The conclusion, the third and last section of your speech, is the place to signal the end is near, to summarize your material, and to leave your audience with something worthwhile and memorable. Let's look at each section of the speech structure in more detail.

The Introduction

An effective introduction should grab the attention of the audience and reveal your specific purpose. If your specific purpose is to persuade your audiences to eat less fat in their diet, a relatively boring introduction would be something like, "This morning I'd like to persuade you to eat less fat in your diet." Ho hum—you probably lost the attention of 80 percent of your audience. The following is a much more interesting introduction:

> Fifty percent of the population of the United States is killing itself. In this room, more than half of us are eating ourselves to an early death brought on by too much fat in our diets. Countless studies indicate that there is a very real relationship between our diet and the development of life-threatening diseases such as cancer, stroke, and diabetes. The *Surgeon General's Report on Nutrition and Health* concurs with this correlation by stating that "The single most influential dietary change one can make to lower the risks of diseases such as cancer, strokes, and diabetes is to reduce intake of foods high in fat."

> Today I stand before you to convince you to reduce your daily intake of fat. I will give you three well-documented reasons that it's important to eat a low-fat diet and then we will look at what a healthy diet looks like. Please attend to my message, as what I say may save your life.

This introduction clearly grabs your attention while also informing you about where the speech is headed. Notice that the introduction also states why the topic is important to the audience. By demonstrating that there is concern about the lives of the audience, the speaker introduces a strong benefit or advantage to the audience. Although the preceding introduction demonstrates one way to get the attention of your audience, several other proven techniques can accomplish the same result. Let's take a closer look at each of these devices for gaining the attention of your audience.

Introduction Techniques

Narratives, statistics, quotations, and rhetorical questions are four devices that are particularly effective in capturing the attention of your audience in the introduction of your speech. You'll begin by looking at one of the most frequently used techniques, the narrative.

Narratives, or brief stories, relate the particulars of an event or occurrence. They are one of the surest ways of gaining and holding your audience's attention. These concrete stories personalize the subject matter by providing information to which people can directly relate. Suppose that you are asked to give a speech on friendship to a local fraternity. You've narrowed your specific purpose to inform your audience about three important qualities a friend should have, basing the information for your speech on your personal experience. Your introduction might be something like this:

> We all remember being in a new situation, one where we were nervous and didn't know anyone. I remember entering a new school in the eleventh grade and feeling that I had no friends at all. But one day, about a month after school had started, I met Ben. Instantly, I identified with his personality, sense of humor, and friendliness, and we became great friends. We spent all of our free time together and in no time at all I knew I was blessed to have such a wonderful pal. We maintained our friendship for ten years, until Ben passed away. Yet before and after his death, he influenced me in countless ways, revealing to me what friendship is all about.

> Today, I would like to share three important lessons Ben taught me about being a true friend. When I am done speaking, you should have a deeper understanding of what true friendship can and should be.

As you can see, this introduction personalized the topic. The speaker turns what could be a somewhat dry and formal subject into an emotional and riveting tale of a personal experience.

Statistics are a second way of attracting and maintaining the attention of your audience. Statistics refer to a collection of quantifiable data. Most people value statistics and put a great deal of credence in them. Suppose that you are to give a speech to a local chapter of female business owners on the future of women in home-based businesses. Your introduction could be something like the following:

> Last year, approximately 45 million Americans worked out of their homes. Approximately half of these people were women, grossing, on the average, $60,000 a year. Within the next ten years, even more Americans will be working out of their homes, with an increase in both the percentage of women and their gross salaries. As women in business, you should be aware of the advantages and disadvantages of operating a home-based business.

> In the next hour, I will provide you with some basic information about the positive and negative aspects of owning a home-based business. The intent of my speech is to share valuable information with you that will result in higher productivity and revenue in your business.

Notice how the preceding introduction uses statistics to relate the subject matter to the audience, gives a succinct overview of the status of home-based businesses, and presents interesting and credible information to the audience.

Quotations, a third device for beginning your speech, are an excellent way to entice your audience to continue to listen. A quotation is the direct use of someone else's words verbatim—exactly as they were said or written. When you quote someone in a speech, or any written work, it is imperative that you acknowledge your source. You need to give credit to the speaker or writer of the passage and you also need to know where to find the quotation in case someone in the audience wants to do further research.

Suppose that you're preparing a speech for your travel club on the importance of understanding and respecting people and cultures of all countries. In your introduction, along with stating your specific purpose and providing your audience with an advantage for listening to your speech, you could cite a world-renowned novelist, James A. Michener, who stated in reference to traveling, "If you reject the food, ignore the customs, fear the religion and avoid the people, you might better stay home." In using Michener's words, you would, of course, relate this quotation to the specific purpose of your speech.

Quotations can come from either experts or peers; you could quote a former president of the United States; a nuclear physicist; or a friend, relative, or classmate. Just make sure that the quotation you use is both relevant to your material and interesting.

A fourth and very effective technique to use in your introduction is a *rhetorical question*. A rhetorical question is not intended to elicit an actual response, but to stimulate your audience to think about the topic. Suppose that you're giving a speech to a small chapter of Mothers Against Drunk Driving about the necessity of more police patrolling on highways after 2 a.m. Your introduction could begin with a rhetorical question such as, "Do you realize that 50 percent of all automobile accidents in our city occur between 2 a.m. and 4 a.m.?" Your intent in asking this rhetorical question is not for the audience to yell out the answer, but rather to reflect on its significance in terms of the content of your speech.

Perhaps you are delivering a persuasive speech to a group of prospective animal owners on the importance of neutering pets. In the introduction of your speech, you could ask a rhetorical question such as, "Are you aware that in the United States, 10 to 25 percent of the pet population is put to death annually? And did you know that each year 10 million dogs and almost 10 million cats are euthanized in animal shelters alone?" Again, your intent is not to have audiences call out a response, but rather to incite them to think. As you can see, rhetorical questions are extremely effective in involving your audiences and securing their attention and interest.

Through the use of narration, statistics, quotations, and rhetorical questions, you can attract the attention of your audiences and create the interest that will keep them attending to your speech. Your audiences will also appreciate a brief overview of where you're headed in your speech and the benefits your material can offer them. Most speech writers agree that it's best to write your introduction last so that you will know all the main points and supporting material in your speech. Because the introduction is the first thing your audience will hear, it's really important to spend time on this part of your speech. By incorporating the techniques in this section, you'll have the knowledge to prepare and deliver a dynamic introduction.

Tips for Preparing an Introduction

1. After you get the attention of the audience, provide an overview of your information and explain why this information is important to the audience.

2. Use quotations that are appropriate to your audience. A quotation from former President Harry Truman would be more appropriate for Democrats than Republicans.

3. Use short sentences in your introduction so that you don't get caught up in verbiage. An outline of sentences or phrases will help you remember important information.

---

4. Don't start out your speech with an apology such as, "I really don't know anything about this," or "I'm so nervous up here." Audiences want you to take command.

5. At the maximum, spend only 30 seconds of a 5-minute speech on your introduction. The introduction is extremely important, but you'll need to spend most of your time on the body of your speech.

6. Relate your topic to the audience. If your research indicates that 25 percent of the population will acquire cancer sometime during their lifetime, you could include a rhetorical question such as, "Do you realize that one out of four people in this room will probably get cancer sometime during his or her life?"

The Body

The body of a speech contains your main points and supporting material or evidence. It is here that you develop your ideas and add depth to your subject matter. For your audience to comprehend and retain your major points, you need to organize your material in a straightforward manner. There are five tried and true patterns of organizing a speech. These patterns, used by successful speakers, are referred to as topical, chronological, spatial, problem-solution, and motivated sequence. Let's examine each pattern in more depth.

Topical Order

The first organizational pattern is topical. Here, you arrange your material based on more specific categories within the subject. For example, if your specific purpose is to inform your audience about three important areas of your life, you might select your religious beliefs, your personal relationship with your significant other, and your pursuit of a degree in higher education as the three main points of your speech. Next, you would determine whether to arrange these topical points in order of most important to least important, from least important to most important, or in points with equal weight. Suppose that you decide to arrange your speech in a topical order with main points from most to least important. Then your outline might look like the following:

Topical Outline

Specific Purpose: To inform my audience about the three major areas of my life.

  I.   The most important area of my life is my love relationship with my significant other.

  II.   The second most important area in my life is my quest for spiritual truth.

  III.   Another instrumental area in my life is my work to acquire a Bachelor of Arts degree.

Of course, you would need to develop each of these main points in depth with subpoints and more detail, but the important lesson is to divide the body of your speech into organized units that are independent yet connected.

Chronological Order

It's important to note that when you organize material in your speech, you can arrange the same subject matter in many different ways. Certain topics lend themselves to various organizational structures, whereas with some material only one organizational structure will work. The important thing is that you select the most comprehensible and retainable format for your information.

Take the same specific purpose used in the preceding topical outline and arrange the subject matter in chronological order. A chronological order would arrange material according to time, either in the order in which it occurred or in reverse chronological order, tracing events backward in time. The following chronological outline lists the important events of the speech writer's life according to the order in which they occurred.

Chronological Outline

Specific Purpose: To inform my audience about the three important areas of my life.

  I.   A spiritual quest became very important to me in high school.

  II.   After I left the service, I became determined to achieve a bachelor of arts degree.

  III.   In college, I developed the love of my life with my significant other.

As you can see, by organizing your subject matter in a chronological pattern, a different speech will emerge. Of course, with whatever organizational pattern you use, it is absolutely essential to develop each of the main points with specific supporting material.

Spatial Order

A third type of organizational pattern that works well in informative speeches is spatial order. In this pattern, you organize the material according to geographical area or space. Suppose that you have been asked to speak to a group of parents about the architectural plans for a new school. The best way to organize the body of your speech is in a spatial order, discussing classroom by classroom, floor by floor, or perhaps area by area. The main points of your speech might look like the following:

Spatial Outline

Specific Purpose: To inform my audience about the four floors of McKinley Junior High School.

    I. The first floor will house the gymnasium, auditorium, cafeteria, and offices.
    II. The second story will contain math and science classes.
    III. The third floor will house the humanities classes.
    IV. The fourth floor will contain the art classes.

You could arrange information in a spatial structure from bottom to top as in the preceding example, from top to bottom, from east to west, from north to south, or from inside to outside. The point is that spatial order provides just another way to separate the units within the body of your speech so that your audience can comprehend and retain the information. As mentioned previously, it is essential to develop each of your main points with supporting materials.

Problem-Solution Order

A fourth organizational pattern is the problem-solution structure. In the body of your speech, you develop two main points: the problem or need section and the solution or satisfaction section. Problem-solution is an excellent organization to use when your general purpose is to persuade rather than to inform or to entertain.

Imagine that you have been asked to speak to your representatives in Congress about the homeless situation in our country. The problem-solution organizational structure would be an excellent pattern to use in your talk. You could begin your speech by establishing the problem or need to do something. In this section, you could develop the problem of the homeless by focusing on the extent of the problem and the reasons that the number of homeless continues to grow. After establishing that there truly is a problem in the United States, you can develop the solution section of your speech. Here, you could focus on an increase of federal social welfare programs, alternatives to the deinstitutionalization of the mentally ill, or whatever you believe are the solutions to the problem. Your main points outline might read as follows:

Problem-Solution Outline

Specific Purpose: To persuade my audience that we need to take legislative action to solve the growing problem of the homeless.

    I. There is a large and growing homeless problem in the United States.

    II. We can solve this problem through a combination of increased federal social welfare programs and decreased deinstitutionalization of the mentally ill.

As in all organizational structures, you need to develop both the problem and solution sections fully with facts, statistics, quotations, and examples. The problem-solution structure provides a relatively simple and effective outline for persuading your audience to take your point of view.

Motivated Sequence Order

The fifth and final organizational pattern, motivated sequence, is also effective when you need to persuade your audience to accept your point of view. This time-honored plan expands on the problem-solution structure by adding three steps so that the sequence looks like the following:

Motivated Sequence Outline

1. Attention
2. Need
3. Satisfaction
4. Visualization
5. Action

Take a closer look at this model by using the homeless material from the preceding problem-solution example. In the *attention* step, you would capture the attention of the audience by focusing on the extent of the homeless problem in the United States through statistics or perhaps a narrative. By stating that conservative estimates of the problem number the homeless at 3 million, and establishing that the problem reaches almost all geographical areas in the United States, your audience's attention is guaranteed.

In moving to the second step, the *need* phase, it is essential to relate the problem to your audience. Here, you could develop the subpoints that because homelessness contributes to a disintegration of the social fabric of our society and to an increase in crime, it affects every member of our population. You can fully support this step with quotations, statistics, or other factual information.

In the third step, the *satisfaction* phase, you focus on a specific, detailed plan that satisfies the need, anticipating and answering any questions your audience may have about the solution. In the homelessness speech, you would explain the federal social welfare programs that you advocate.

The fourth step, *visualization*, envisions what the situation would be like when your solution is accepted or enacted. You could examine the positive results in another country that has a similar type of social welfare program or you could hypothesize what the United States would be like if the programs you advocate are enacted.

The final step, *action*, is just as the name implies. It's this step that results in the total involvement of your audience to do or believe something. In the homelessness speech, you would move your audience (Congress) to enact legislation aimed at more social welfare programs.

The motivated sequence is more complex than the other organizational patterns, but it is a highly effective structure to use in persuasive talks as well as in other forms of communication intended to persuade. The main points of the homelessness speech would look like the following:

Motivated Sequence Outline

Specific Purpose: To persuade my audience to enact more federal social welfare programs for the homeless.

   I. The extent of the homeless situation in the United States is alarming. (Attention)
  II. We are all affected by this serious problem. (Need)
 III. The solution to the homeless problem is an increase in federal aid. (Satisfaction)
  IV. By looking at federal social welfare programs for the homeless in Canada, we can see how beneficial such programs would be in the United States. (Visualization)
   V. You must act now by enacting specific legislation for the homeless. (Action)

This section discussed five important patterns of organization for the body of your speech. By using topical, chronological, spatial, problem-solution, or the motivated sequence, you are taking one more step toward mastering the organization of your speech.

The Conclusion

The conclusion of your speech serves three functions: to signal that the end of your speech is near, to summarize your material, and to leave your audience with something memorable and worthwhile. Many studies indicate that although the conclusion is the last thing your audience hears, it may be the first thing that they remember. So it is extremely important that you deliver an impressive conclusion.

There are three techniques that you can use to create an effective conclusion. These devices include the use of a quotation, narration, and challenges or appeals. Let's take a look at each of these.

Quotations can be a memorable way to end your speech. Suppose that you are concluding your motivational talk about the importance of positive thinking. The following could be an effective way to end your speech:

> Over the last hour, I have demonstrated how positive thinking leads to positive results in every aspect of one's life. We have examined research, testimonials, and personal stories that indicate the truth of this belief. Now, I'll close my speech with a quotation from an American entrepreneur, Mary Kay Ash, who built a multimillion-dollar cosmetic company. According to Mary Kay, "If you think you can, you can. And if you think you can't, you're right." Remember that positive thinking can work for you. Thank you and good night.

In addition to using quotations from experts, you can also include a quotation from a friend or classmate as long as the quotation summarizes the essence of what you are talking about. Also remember to give credit where credit is due and cite who stated the quotation.

Through the use of *narration*, telling a story to your audience, you can personalize your material and create a conclusion with great impact. Examine how you can use a narrative in the final portion of your speech. Imagine that you are the director of the local branch of the Barbara Bush Foundation for Family Literacy, the volunteer reading program established by the former first lady in 1989. In a persuasive speech about the program, given to prospective volunteers, you decide to use narration in your conclusion. You could use the following example to end your speech.

> Over the last hour, I've spent our time together discussing why you should become involved with the Barbara Bush Foundation for Family Literacy. We've examined the facts and statistics that indicate that something must be done to rid our country of illiteracy.

We've discussed ways that you can help others to learn to read, and we've seen how volunteers, like yourselves, are truly responsible for the success of the program. Before you leave this evening, I would like to share the story of someone whose life was dramatically altered because of her relationship with a volunteer from the Barbara Bush Foundation for Family Literacy.

Heather spent the majority of her twenty-nine years of life in dead-end jobs or being unemployed. Because school had never been a priority, she was a fourth-grade dropout, unable to read or plan the type of future she dreamed of.

Then, one day her world changed. A volunteer from the Barbara Bush Foundation for Family Literacy introduced her to the world of words, books, written fantasies, and success stories. After two years, Heather mastered reading skills, received a high-school equivalency degree, and was able to become employed in an entry-level position in a bank. Heather's life was transformed because of a volunteer and the Family Literacy program.

Think about all that I've shared with you this evening and please become a volunteer so that we can help millions of people like Heather. Thank you very much for your time and attention.

Another effective way to end your speech is through the use of a *challenge* or *appeal*. This is a particularly functional device to use when you are persuading your audience to change a belief, action, or attitude. The following conclusion is an excerpt from a speech to persuade the audience to lobby for efficient disposal of radioactive waste:

As my speech draws to an end, I'd like to reiterate a few main points of my speech. We have examined in depth one of our world's most serious problems: radioactive waste. We've learned that the byproducts of nuclear weaponry and nuclear-power generation are increasing and can remain lethal for thousands of years. We know that nuclear waste is now being stored in temporary sites and that Congress has future plans for storing highly radioactive waste underground, but, as we've learned today, we must act now.

I am requesting that after this speech, each of you think about what I have said this afternoon. Take some time and read the literature that will be distributed at the door. Do some research on the extent of nuclear waste. Discuss this situation with your friends and family. Then, if you decide that there is a real and clear problem with nuclear waste, act.

Write your representatives in Congress, develop and distribute a petition, or protest at nuclear energy plants. My final request is that all of you, to whatever extent you can, do something about nuclear waste because it's a problem that won't go away unless we act, and act now. Thank you.

Whether you use quotations, narration, a challenge, or another device in your conclusion, remember to develop interesting and noteworthy final remarks. Also remember that the last thing you say may be the first thing your audience recalls.

Tips for Writing a Conclusion

1. Use a written outline of brief phrases or simple sentences for your conclusion, but don't read it verbatim. Work on eye contact instead.

2. Your conclusion is the place to summarize and leave your audience with something memorable, so never introduce new main points.

3. There's nothing worse than when a speaker's conclusion simply states, "That's it." Spending time on the preparation of your speech should result in more sophisticated final remarks.

4. It's effective to tie your conclusion to your introduction in some way. If you've used a narrative about someone in the introduction, perhaps you could mention the same person again in the conclusion. Your objective is to create a cohesive unit within the three parts of your speech.

TRANSITIONS

Because it's virtually impossible to keep an audience totally engaged throughout a long speech and because it's so very important to tie the three parts of your speech together, most speakers use transitions to keep the audience tuned in and to connect the ideas in their talk. Transitions are words, phrases, or sentences that show relationships between ideas. You can use transitions to join the introduction, body, and conclusion and to cohere ideas within one of the three parts of your speech. Some of the most frequently used transitions include signposts, internal previews, internal reviews, and summaries.

Signposts connect ideas and help to keep your audience on track. During a speech covering the six benefits of exercise, a member of the audience may begin daydreaming (as research indicates that most audiences do at some time during a speech). By interjecting signposts, such as *first*, *second*, and *third* throughout your talk, you can assist your audience to stay with you and on target. Some of the most frequently used signposts are the following:

- Let's discuss the three benefits . . .
- First . . . Second . . . Third . . . Last, or Firstly . . . Secondly . . . Thirdly . . . Lastly
- Specifically . . .
- Now let's examine the most important reason . . .
- What happened next?
- Further . . .
- Consider these two alternatives . . .
- In the first place . . . In the second place . . .

A second type of transition is the *internal preview*. Internal previews prepare your audience for forthcoming information. For example, in a speech on the influence of A. Milne's classic story *Winnie-the-Pooh*, you could use an internal preview like the following:

> Let's examine the second impact of *Winnie-the-Pooh*. In this portion of my speech, I will discuss how this delightful book has influenced children's literature, children's films, and children's video games.

The *internal review* provides your audience with a summary of your information before you move on to new ideas. Internal reviews assist your audience in retaining important points. For example, at the end of the first main point of a speech to inform a group of expectant mothers about early development of visual and auditory skills, you could say,

> "Over the last hour, we have examined when most babies develop sight, depth perception, and eye and hand coordination. We have also looked at ways to maximize your baby's development in these areas." In essence, a review sums up what you have said before you move on to another point.

There's a commonly used and truthful saying in speech: An effective speech tells the audience what they're going to hear, what they're hearing, and what they've heard. Internal previews and reviews definitely assist in accomplishing this goal.

The final transition is the *summary*. Instead of stating the overly used phrase, "In conclusion," try to develop more innovative ways to signal that the end of your speech is near. The following list of summaries may give you some good ideas about how to wrap up your speech:

- Therefore . . .
- In summary . . .
- Before I leave you today . . .
- Now that I've almost completed my speech . . .

Signposts, internal previews, internal reviews, and summaries assist your audience to stay involved and aware of where you are, where you've been, and where you're headed. When you use transitions, you're creating a more organized speech and essentially taking one more step toward becoming a more effective speaker.

SUMMARY

Organization has been this chapter's major focus. The chapter covered the purpose of the three parts of a speech: the introduction, body, and conclusion. You also examined five important organizational patterns, as well as the function and use of transitions. Recognizing and incorporating this material into your speechmaking skills will result in more organized and, consequently, more effective speeches.

Chapter Three

Using Evidence

Annie Mack thought that she was fully prepared when she stood in front of her city council. She had the best of intentions and the support of more than 300 written names on a petition urging the city council to build a library. And yet when she was finally given the opportunity to speak, she was met with skeptical glances and blank stares. What happened? Annie began her speech with a dramatic introduction that both grabbed the city council's attention and outlined her persuasive purpose of convincing the council of the importance of building a new library. Then she moved into the body of her speech and made many assertions—declarations that certain ideas are true—without any supporting material. Annie made such statements as, "The majority of people in our city need and want a library," "It's important for the welfare of our children to have a library," and "I think that a library will help us remember our past."

Unfortunately, Annie didn't support her assertions with evidence such as quotations, statistics, or narratives. To convince the city council, she should have stated assertions and then supported them with evidence, as in the following examples:

> The majority of people in our community need and want a library in our city. In a recent survey conducted by the *Marion News*, 85 percent of our citizens said that they wanted a library. To pay for the building, 90 percent of Marion's adult population supports an increase in taxes.

> It's important for the welfare of our children and future generations to have a library. The Marion Teachers Association concurs and has issued a declaration stating, "Test scores of the children of Marion are below the national average and unless we can provide more reading materials in a library, a continual decline in scores will most surely continue."

> Libraries enable us to communicate through distance and time with the living and the dead. They enable us to understand our world and our past. In the words of George Santayana, author of *The*

Life of Reason, "Those who cannot remember the past are condemned to repeat it."

Notice how the inclusion of evidence creates more credible reasons that the city council should support a new library. Through the incorporation of verbal support in the form of statistics and quotations, Annie was able to rely on sources outside of herself and thus form a more believable and effective argument.

Evidence, also defined as supporting material, can accomplish several things in your speech. It can prove an assertion or claim that you've made, clarify a concept, reinforce an idea, create a more interesting speech, and increase your credibility as a speaker. Most audiences analyze the effectiveness of an argument based on the quality and quantity of evidence provided, so don't neglect to include evidence in your speech. As you become more proficient at incorporating evidence into your own speeches, you will also become a better critic for evaluating evidence in the speeches and writings of others. This heightened skill will assist your own speaking and writing and also assist you in your lifelong pursuit of truth.

This chapter examines four types of evidence you can use: quotations, statistics, narratives, and definitions. You'll look at pragmatic and helpful examples and tips so that you will fully understand and appreciate the value of evidence.

QUOTATIONS

Quotations refer to the cited words of a peer, expert, or eyewitness who has had experience in the area you are discussing. Quotations can clarify, prove, or expand on an assertion that you make. If you are giving a speech on commercial real estate in New York, a quotation from Donald Trump would probably be quite useful. Or if you plan to discuss the women's movement of the 1970s, Gloria Steinem most definitely had something worthwhile to say about it. A veterinarian might have the quintessential quotation about the importance of neutering your pet, and a survivor of a major airplane crash would certainly be able to tell you what she experienced. The point is that we all can't be experts in all areas of life, so we need to find someone who knows more about a specific topic than we do. The following list of assertions and quotations should clarify how you can use someone else's words:

Assertions and Quotations

Assertion: Many great scientists noted the importance of spirituality in their work and lives.

Quotation: Albert Einstein, one of the greatest physicists of all time, stated on April 18, 1955, that "the cosmic religious experience is the strongest and the noblest driving force behind scientific research."

Assertion: I think that people become stronger individuals as they work through their problems.

Quotation: According to Dr. M. Scott Peck, psychologist and author of the best-selling book *The Road Less Traveled*, "It is only because of problems that we grow mentally and spiritually."

Assertion: We must all have goals in our lives.

Quotation: Benjamin E. Mays, former President of Morehouse College, once stated, "The tragedy of life doesn't lie in not reaching your goal. The tragedy lies in having no goal to reach."

Assertion: Being an unwed teenage mother is a difficult position to be in.

Quotation: Kathy Lynn, 17 years old, unmarried, and the mother of a seven-month-old boy, states, "I thought that my life as a mother would be easy. Now I know that being a mother involves sleepless nights, unlimited patience, and an incredible amount of responsibility."

By using a quotation to support an assertion, you will provide powerful and colorful evidence for your audience. The following list of tips should help you when using quotations.

Tips for Using Quotations

1. Try to use a brief quotation when you're reading verbatim. Long quotations will try your audience's patience.

2. Carefully examine whether to paraphrase a quotation or read it word for word. The quotation and the context within your speech should dictate how you should use the quotation.

3. Always be able to provide when a quotation was spoken or written. If you don't include the citation in your speech, someone may ask for this information during a question and answer period.

4. Make sure that you quote someone who is an expert or has experienced something directly related to your topic. Whoopi Goldberg may be an expert in comedy, but not necessarily in the dwindling rain forests.

STATISTICS

Statistics refer to facts that can be stated in numbers. Statistics are a collection of quantifiable data that can clarify, reinforce, or prove your assertions. Instead of stating that, "The number of families classified as officially poor increased last year," you could state that, "According to the United States Bureau of Census, the number of officially poor people increased by 613,000 over the last year." Or rather than saying, "The average cost of a home in America is a lot," you could state that, "According to the latest *Almanac Please*, the average cost of an American home is $110,000." Statistics give the audience specific and credible information to support your claims.

Examine the following list of assertions and supporting statistics. Notice how even a broad assertion can become clear and understandable.

Assertions and Statistics

Assertion: Most Americans are Protestant, whereas the Jewish faith is the least represented in America.

Statistic: Sixty-one percent of all Americans are Protestant, making it the largest religion in the United States. Two percent of all Americans are Jewish, making it the smallest religion in the United States.

Assertion: The size of the United States is pretty small compared to the rest of the world.

Statistic: Although the United States is approximately 3,800,000 square miles, its share of the world land mass is only 6 percent.

Assertion: The winter temperatures in Phoenix are mild, whereas the summers are extremely hot.

Statistic: Although the average temperature in Phoenix in January is a mild 65 degrees Fahrenheit, by June the average temperature is 100 degrees Fahrenheit.

Assertion: Do you realize that you have to work several months to pay your annual taxes?

Statistic: Did you know that the average American citizen must work from January 1 through May 3, or 123 days, to pay off federal, state, and local taxes?

As you can see from the preceding examples, you can use statistics to clarify, reinforce, and prove your claims. Most speakers and writers have learned the important lesson that statistics are a great asset in building an argument.

The following list of tips will assist you in your use of statistics:

Tips for Using Statistics

1. Relate your statistics to your audience. If it's possible, personalize your numbers. If you state that "Research has shown that one out of every three people in this classroom will score over 90 percent on this exam," your audience will be more directly involved in your speech.

2. Round off your numbers. Isn't it easier for both you and your audience to remember 5,000,000 rather than 4,898,112?

3. Don't lump an excessive number of statistics together. It's overload to state that, "According to the U.S. Bureau of Census, the average poverty threshold for a family of four was $13,924 last year. Average poverty for a person living alone is $6,900 whereas $28,000 is the threshold for a family of nine. Some 35.7 million Americans were considered poor in 1996, a 613,000 person increase over 1995."

4. Maximize the effectiveness of your statistics through separation and explanation of them. After presenting statistical data, take the time to explain their significance to your audience before jumping to the next set of figures. Remember you're a person, not an almanac.

5. Make sure that you are using statistics that are accurate. You are responsible for their accuracy, so check the source and, when possible, the study behind the statistics.

6. Always know the source of your statistics. Your audience may want to do additional research and will need to know where to get the information. If you are unable to give the full citation for your statistic within your speech, have a bibliography available for your audience.

NARRATION

One of the most effective forms of evidence is narration—telling a story about a person, event, or a situation. Because narration is a concrete, personal-interest story, your audience can relate directly to what you say, and you can keep them engaged while you support your main points. Norman Vincent Peale, author of the best-seller, *The Power of Positive Thinking*, said his favorite form of supporting material was narration, because it was most likely to keep the audience's attention. Peale, who was also a popular and influential preacher, recommended using several narratives to support each main point. Although usually it is better to incorporate a variety of evidence into your speech, narration is a highly effective form of support.

Dale Carnegie, author and creator of the Dale Carnegie Course in Public Speaking and Human Relations, also advocated the use of personal interest stories in speeches. He advised his students to use concrete and visual stories, covering the essentials of who, what, where, and when, while being careful not to overload the audience with too much detail. You should use narration to substantiate your main points, not to replace them in your audience's memory.

There are two major types of narration: brief and detailed. The brief form of narration covers the essential facts of the story, telling who, what, and when. Because of its abbreviated form, the brief narration tells a succinct and simple story. The detailed form does what its name implies—it adds more detail to tell how the story unfolded. Note also that both brief and detailed narratives can be either factual (true) or hypothetical (uncertain or fictitious). So there are essentially the following four types of narration:

- Brief factual narration
- Detailed factual narration
- Brief hypothetical narration
- Detailed hypothetical narration

Now take a closer look at each of these four types of narration, beginning with the brief factual narration. Each example presents an assertion, supporting it with a different type of narration.

Assertion and Brief Factual Narration

Assertion: The American West was settled by many adventurous and courageous women.

Brief Factual Narration: One of the most adventurous and courageous individuals to settle the American West was a woman named Nellie Cashman. In the late 1880s, Nellie lived in various areas of Arizona, working as a miner and eventually operating eleven mines and several grocery stores. She was, as the *Tucson Daily Star* so aptly stated in October of 1895, "one of the most extraordinary women in America."

Assertion and Detailed Factual Narration

Assertion: The American West was settled by many adventurous and courageous women.

Detailed Factual Narration: The American West of the late 1880s was a tough and dangerous place to live. Famine, drought, disease, and battles with Indians were just a few of the problems that prevailed in this unknown region. During this formative period of the western frontier, there were many individuals whose lives were based on courage and discovery. One of these heroes was a woman whose name was Nellie Cashman.

Between 1880 and 1900, Nellie Cashman lived in many parts of Arizona. She spent ten years as a miner, crossing the desert on foot, with only a burro to carry her precious water and food. Nellie was an attractive, strong, and determined woman who eventually owned eleven mines and several grocery stores. Her life revolved around travel, philanthropic interests, and risk-taking entrepreneurial endeavors.

In fact, in October of 1895, the *Tucson Daily Star* referred to Nellie as "one of the most extraordinary women in America."

Her zest for life is so aptly revealed in some of her final words. "You never quite know," Nellie mused as she approached the end of her years, "what's going to happen next, or when your time will come to cash in your checks. It all adds interest and variety to life."

Assertion and Brief Hypothetical Narration

Assertion: Personal obsessions can lead to a daunting experience.

Brief Hypothetical Narration: Imagine that one evening you discover that someone has left an anonymous love note on your e-mail. The next day an unfamiliar voice telephones to confess love for you. Soon unsigned notes are left on your windshield and front door and a strange figure is seen viewing your apartment from across the street. Your pleas to the police go unanswered and the number of the obsessional contacts increases.

Someone is becoming more desperate in a confession of love. And as a result, you too are becoming more desperate—desperate for a solution to this problem. Welcome to the world of personal obsession, a world, according to psychologists, that is growing dramatically in America.

Assertion and Detailed Hypothetical Narration

Assertion: Personal obsessions can lead to a daunting experience.

Detailed Hypothetical Narration: Imagine that one day, after spending eight hours at work, you come home and decide to spend an hour or so cruising the Web. Your delight to find some e-mail turns into disappointment when you conclude that a love note was sent to you accidentally. Later that same evening, you receive a couple of weird phone calls from someone of the opposite sex who confesses love for you.

The next morning there's a package and unsigned note outside your front door. Things become even more intense when you arrive at work to find another present and a note with accusations of unreturned love. The source of this unknown fixation accelerates contact and you are bombarded with more e-mail, telephone calls, letters, and packages. The police say there's nothing they can do at this point, and your fears escalate.

Over the next two weeks, things continue to accelerate until one night, on returning home late from an evening class, you see someone hiding behind a shrub in front of your house, waiting for you. You freeze, unable to see if your stalker is armed.

Welcome to contemporary society, a time when stalkings have soared and psychologists have become genuinely concerned about the phenomenon of personal obsessions.

As you can see, narration clearly succeeds at holding the attention of an audience. In all forms of narration—brief factual, detailed factual, brief hypothetical, and detailed hypothetical—these personalized accounts are extremely effective forms of evidence to use in your speech.

DEFINITIONS

Definitions, a fourth form of evidence, are particularly important when you're explaining vague, foreign, technical, or unfamiliar terms. For example, you could say that you are pro-choice (in favor of abortion), but what exactly do you mean? Do you support abortion in all cases only through the first trimester of a pregnancy or through the second trimester? Perhaps you are pro-choice only when a pregnancy occurs as a result of a rape or incest? Clarification by means of a definition would clearly explain your use of the vague term, pro-choice.

You also need to define foreign and technical words with which your audience may be unfamiliar. When encouraging your audiences to try a chimichanga when they travel in Arizona or New Mexico, make sure to let them know that they'll be ordering a deep-fried tortilla wrapped around a filling with meat, beans, and/or cheese. Or when you mention an epidural anesthesia in a speech on your wife's birthing experience, inform your audience that this is an injection of a local anesthetic into the lower region of the spine. It's also best to give the definition when you first mention the term rather than to wait until the question-and-answer period following your talk. That way you can make sure that you and your audience are on the same wavelength.

A third occasion to define a term is when you use an acronym—a word formed from the initial letters of a name. When using the acronym WAC in your speech on famous women in the military, it is best to define the term as Women's Army Corps. Don't expect your audience to be as familiar as you are with specialized terms.

When you use definitions as evidence in your speeches, the following tips will help your audience to grasp the information.

Tips for Using Definitions

1. It's best to paraphrase rather than read a lengthy definition from a dictionary. Personalize the definition by putting it in your own words.

2. If you have found conflicting definitions, cite the source of the one you are using.

3. You should offer a definition the first time you use a word. Don't wait until you've used the word three times and already confused your audience.

Whether you use quotations, statistics, narration, or definitions as supporting material, ask yourself the following questions during the writing phase of your speech:

Questions About Your Evidence

- Do I have enough evidence to defend my assertion, or do I need to gather more supporting material?
- Have I explained my evidence clearly?
- Is my evidence taken from an unbiased and credible source?
- Is my evidence current?

SUMMARY

This chapter covered the four basic types of evidence: quotations, statistics, narration, and definitions. The chapter's focus has been on the practical use of each type of supporting material so that you can create a more credible and interesting speech. Throughout, the chapter has also emphasized that the more time you put into the preparation of your assertions and evidence, the more likely your audience will be to accept what you say. So carefully prepare your evidence, and move one step closer to becoming an effective speaker.

Chapter Four

Research and Documentation

As soon as Molly Cadigan received her speech assignment, she knew what her specific purpose would be. She decided that she would persuade her audience that annulment in the Roman Catholic Church is a hypocrisy and should be disallowed. Molly selected a topic in which she strongly believed and with which she had a personal experience. When Molly was 12 years old, her father petitioned the Roman Catholic Church for an annulment. She experienced firsthand her mother's trauma as wounds from the divorce three years prior were reopened. At 12, Molly felt this situation was not right, and now, at 20, she decided to prove that annulment was not ethically, spiritually, or morally correct.

Molly also knew that although her strong belief was a great motivator for writing and delivering her speech, she would still need to find a lot of evidence to support her assertions. Molly recognized that she would need to do *research*—careful and deliberate investigation and inquiry—to find her supporting material. Molly decided to vary her supporting material by doing both primary and secondary research into her topic. Primary research would involve finding evidence on her own through conducting interviews or administering surveys, whereas secondary research would involve the examination of previously published materials such as journals, magazines, books, and videotapes.

Molly would document all sources of evidence by writing down pertinent information about each one. Through *documentation* (verification of the source of the information), Molly could keep a complete account of what she found and where she found it. This process would help her not only as she wrote her speech but also when it was time to prepare her bibliography.

Like Molly, you'll need to become proficient at doing research and documentation. These two skills will assist you not only with your academic work, but also with finding out the safest car to drive, what's happening in real estate trends, how to prevent certain diseases, or other practical information that you may need throughout your life.

This chapter begins by discussing primary research, then covers secondary research. Finally, you'll take a look at documentation. It's important to note that although research and documentation can be exciting and most interesting, they can also be quite challenging. So keep the faith when you're looking for evidence and remember that your hard work will always pay off.

INTERVIEWS

One of the most interesting ways of gathering current information is by interviewing people. If you're preparing a speech on the recycling problem in your city, perhaps an interview with a representative from the local waste-management business would be helpful. Who better to explain his theory on the decline in SAT scores than one of the test founders? The quickest way to find out whether your mayor plans to run for office may be to call his assistant. The bottom line is that sometimes it is in the best interest of your speech to rely on a brief telephone inquiry or a lengthy face-to-face interview for essential information.

If you decide that a face-to-face interview is the best way to gather research, and you're still looking for an ideal source, then the telephone book is a good place to begin. Most businesses and associations will have a spokesperson who will address any question or concern. These people will probably have brochures, pamphlets, reports, or other materials that may be of use to you. You'll just need to ask for them. *The Encyclopedia of Associations* is also an excellent reference book that lists groups around the country.

The interview begins when you make the first contact with the interviewee. Treat people as you want to be treated. When telephoning for an interview, remember that a succinct and polite introduction will increase the chances that your request will be granted. Always identify yourself and be specific about what you want to know and where you will use the information. Make sure that you have plenty of available times to meet with the person, just in case she or he has only one or two available times to meet with you. Scheduling a half-hour session should be enough time to conduct an interview. Also request any biographical or other written materials before you actually meet. This will give your interviewee time to put together some important documents that will probably be quite useful down the road.

When you arrive at your interview, repeat your name, what your speech is about, and what information you're looking for. Don't expect the person to remember anything about you; be polite and save her or him the embarrassment of asking you those questions.

Make sure that you have at least ten thought-provoking questions written out or memorized. If you want specific information, you'll need to take command of the interview. Throughout the interview, be a great listener. Develop eye contact, nod at appropriate places, and ask for clarification when you don't understand something. Don't speak any more than one-fifth of the time during the interview. You're there to receive information, not to lecture.

Bring along an audiotape recorder, and if your interviewee doesn't object, tape record your interview. Because you won't have to concentrate on writing down every word, you'll be a better listener who can key in to something really important your interviewee has to say. Always make sure that you have tapes and new batteries, and that your recorder is working properly. If you do end up taking notes, work out a system of shorthand, because writing down every word could take up too much time.

The following list of interview tips will assist you in your quest for information:

Tips for Interviewing

1. Ask open-ended questions. Rather than asking when a scientist's work began, you can request that the scientist tell you about her early research.

2. At the same time, remember to be focused. If you state, "Tell me about your life," you may never get the specific information you are looking for.

3. Stay on one track of questioning at a time. If you ask, "Please explain the theory behind your clinical work and what do you plan to do with your writing?" the result will be two lines of answers.

4. If you disagree with interviewees, challenge them by saying, "Let me play the devil's advocate," then state your position. Remember, you don't want to alienate your experts.

5. Give your interviewee time to answer your questions. Don't be too quick to prove your brilliance by jumping in with another question.

6. At the end of the interview, review your questions to make sure you covered everything and that you fully understand the information. Give your interviewee a chance to have the last word by asking if he or she wants to add anything.

7. Make sure to thank your interviewee for his or her time, and send a thank-you note a day or so after the interview.

SURVEYS

An excellent way to get your audience involved in your speech is by administering a survey. Surveys provide a general or comprehensive view of what a group of people think, believe, or know about something. Surveys can run the gamut from a lengthy pretest administered to your audience to an informal request for a show of hands. In preparation for your speech on a campus policy, why not talk to some of your classmates and find out how they feel about the issue? If you've been asked to speak about investing in mutual funds to a club made up of strangers, perhaps it would be in your best interest to send out a questionnaire to determine exactly what your audience already knows about these funds. Before you prepare your speech on ways to reduce credit card debt, you could poll your audience to find out if the respondents do in fact use their credit cards, and if so, what kind of interest and debt they have secured. It's always important to guard the privacy of your respondents by ensuring that all answers remain anonymous. Results from peer surveys and interviews serve two purposes: They help you to focus on specific material in your speech, and they secure the attention of your audiences, because the data came from them.

COMPUTER SEARCHES

Over the last twenty years, there have been dramatic changes in the world of computers. One place where new computer technology has had a huge impact is in the organization of information in libraries. Now almost all libraries are equipped with computer catalogs that can perform an information search in a matter of minutes. Twenty years ago, a similar search may have taken hours or even days to complete.

Today, computer searches use a variety of electronic databases, such as the Magazine Index, Expanded Academic Index, the Business Index, and thousands of others. There are also CD-ROM reference materials that contain periodical indexes, abstract summaries, and full texts of books, periodicals, and nonprint media. There are even Web sites such as the Electric Library that display the full text of over 800 publications. Because the world of computer technology for research is changing so rapidly, you may want to attend a computer instruction session at your library or school. You can also stay current about new research sites by reading articles in current computer periodicals.

Although the type and quantity of computer catalogs and CD-ROM reference materials vary from library to library, use is quick and simple. You can access information with two basic instructions: You search for material by author, title, or subject, and you limit your topic to find the most relevant information. Instead of using a broad term such as "nonverbal communication in speech" and receiving hundreds of articles, you can narrow your topic to "eye contact or gestures." You can always add other key words later. Narrowing your topic will help you to keep focused and get started with a manageable amount of material.

As you research your topic, it is extremely important that you keep accurate and complete records of what you've read. Write down the title, author, publication information, page number, and a summary, quotation, or a paraphrase of that source's relevant material. Record your information on notecards or notebook paper, or into your computer. It's always a good idea to be able to arrange and rearrange your research cards in various organizational patterns later. Remember to place quotation marks around quotations and verbatim passages from your source and always jot down a page number, because you may need it later.

Although computer searches are a quick and easy method for securing all the evidence you need for your speech, you should still be aware of some of the more important reference materials in print. Knowledge of these materials will help you to know what's available and where you can find it.

LIBRARY REFERENCE MATERIALS

Most libraries spend a great deal of money on current noncirculating books for their reference section. There are many books that provide an overview of your topic, whereas others present more detailed information. In addition to general encyclopedias such as *Collier's Encyclopedia* or *Encyclopedia Britannica*, there are specialized encyclopedias such as the *Encyclopedia of Music, Encyclopedia of Theatre*, and *Encyclopedia of Space*. There are also interesting illustrated encyclopedias such as *How It Works*, which, in 22 volumes, explains a multitude of science and technology processes in simple terms. Browse in the encyclopedia section of your library or ask the reference librarian for an appropriate title that covers your topic.

Dictionaries also range from the general to the highly specific. Most libraries carry *Webster's International Dictionary* while also handling dictionaries such as *The Dictionary of Social Sciences, The Dictionary of Drugs,* and *The Dictionary of Art*. There is also a *Dictionary of Foreign Phrases and Abbreviations* that lists common phrases in French, German, Greek, and Hebrew translated into English. These more specialized dictionaries provide in-depth articles that are unavailable in more generalized publications.

The reference section of your library is also a great place to go if you're looking for information about a specific person. Consult texts such as *Dictionary of American Biography, Current Biography,* or *Who's Who in America* to give you the quintessential information about a particular individual.

The reference section also houses some useful almanacs and yearbooks that are excellent sources of statistics and facts. Check with your reference librarian for books such as *Facts on File, Statistical Abstracts of the United States, The World Almanac and Book of Facts, Editorials on File, The Annual Register: World Events in . . . , Congressional Quarterly Almanac, U.S. Supreme Court Reports Lawyer's Edition,* and *Standard and Poor's Register of Corporations, Directors, and Executives.*

Facts on File summarizes and indexes the news each week, providing factual, up-to-date accounts of current events, national and foreign news, science, sports, medicine, education, religion, crime, books, plays, films, and people. *Statistical Abstracts of the United States*, published annually by the United States government, is a good place to look when you need statistics. It compiles tables on social, political, and economic issues in the United States, based on census reports. *The World Almanac and Book of Facts* contains a variety of general information, including astronomical and meteorological data, whereas *Editorials on File* reprints editorials on a variety of subjects that were published in newspapers from across the country. It is an excellent place to find pro and con arguments for a topic. *The Annual Register: World Events In . . .* is a collection of current articles on events, countries, regions, and institutions. The articles are several pages long and are more general than those in *Facts on File.*

If you are doing research on federal legislation, you may want to examine the *Congressional Quarterly Almanac*, as it is a digest of major legislation in Congress during the year. Under each topic, this book summarizes and reviews Congressional debate on each relevant piece of legislation, committee action, and action on the floor. *U.S. Supreme Court Reports Lawyer's Edition* examines judicial cases. It lists brief summaries and texts of decisions in cases heard by the U.S. Supreme Court since 1754.

Finally, *Standard and Poor's Register of Corporations, Directors, and Executives* is an annual publication listing addresses and phone numbers as well as officers, number of employees, and yearly sales figures for nearly 40,000 American corporations.

If you're looking for a specific quotation, check the library. Some of the many sources that deal with quotations include *Bartlett's Familiar Quotations, Oxford Dictionary of Quotations,* and *The Home Book of Quotations.* There's even a book of quotations entitled *Shakespeare's Insults!*

As you can see by the previously mentioned sampling of materials, reference books are varied and numerous, specific and general, and contemporary and dated. They are exciting places to search for evidence, and you'll never have to worry about their availability, because patrons cannot check them out of the library.

PERIODICALS—NEWSPAPERS, MAGAZINES, AND JOURNALS

You can find a great deal of valuable and easily accessible information in periodicals. Periodicals are newspapers, magazines, and journals that contain current information on a variety of subjects. Whereas books provide more depth in covering a topic, periodicals are the place to go to find timely information. Newspapers are daily or weekly accounts of current events. Your library should subscribe to important national newspapers such as the *New York Times* and the *Los Angeles Times* as well as your local newspaper.

Magazines are written for a general audience by professional writers and include titles such as *Time, Newsweek, Forbes, Rolling Stone,* and *Sports Illustrated.* Journals or scholarly magazines cover specialized disciplines and are written by experts in that field. Examples of journals include the *Journal of the American Medical Association, Journal of Applied Psychology,* and *Harvard Business Review.* Magazine articles are generally written in straightforward, popular language, whereas journals tend to be more technical and academic, because they target experts in the field.

Libraries subscribe to periodicals in forms such as the original individual printed form, hardbound volumes of the printed form, microfiche (a flat, filmed copy of a publication read on a microfiche printer), microfilm (film reproduction of a printed publication stored on a reel and read on a microfilm printer), and CD-ROM or electronic databases. To find a specific article in one of these forms, you need to search an index that specifies where to go.

Indexes are hardbound books, paperback sources, or electronic databases that contain citations (descriptions of published works that give such particulars as authorship, title, edition, date, and pages) that you can access by looking up topics alphabetically. There are general indexes, such as *The Reader's Guide to Periodical Literature,* that list articles from more than 200 magazines. And there are indexes for newspapers such as *The New York Times Index* and *The Wall Street Journal Index.* There are also very specialized indexes that catalog articles about particular disciplines, such as nursing, psychology, or business. You access these indexes by narrowing your topic and then selecting articles you want to examine. Always write down the complete citation and any information you receive from that source. As you've already learned, your citations are valuable information that you need to keep.

ELECTRONIC MEDIA

Research indicates that most Americans credit television and cable as their primary source of news. Although this fact may or may not be surprising to you, it does mean that the electronic media (cable, television, radio, videotape, and film) have infiltrated our lives and are rapidly becoming larger sources of information for your research.

If you were doing research on whales in the Arctic Ocean, you could look at a video documentary on whales produced by the Public Broadcasting Corporation or the Discovery Channel. Perhaps you listened to a radio interview with the director of a local domestic abuse center and you want to use the information in your speech on domestic violence. These might be relevant and interesting sources of evidence for your speech. Your library will also have an index of its electronic media holdings, so check with your librarian if you're unsure of how to locate the information.

Whether you do your research in electronic media or another source, there are a few research tips that will help you to gather credible and important evidence. The following list will guide you through your research.

Tips for Conducting Research

1. Begin your research early. This is a hard but very important lesson to learn. The earlier you start to think about your topic, conduct research, and prepare your supporting materials, the more time you'll have to write and rehearse your speech. Research generally takes much longer than most people anticipate.

2. Become an expert in research, search out the reference librarian, or make friends with someone who knows about research. The more information you can sift through, the more knowledgeable you'll be, and the stronger the evidence you decide to use will be too.

3. Write down the citation of your sources immediately. That way you'll have all of the information available when you need it.

4. Use a variety of sources (if they're available). You should rely on books, magazine articles, and reference materials for each speech. A variety of sources will provide you with a broader perspective on a topic.

DOCUMENTING YOUR RESEARCH

As you gather your research materials, remember to document each source of information you use. Always record a citation—a written account of the author, title, date of publication, volume, and page number—along with a summary of the material. You will arrange all your citations later in alphabetical order for a *bibliography*—a written compilation of your sources of information. Although all bibliographies are arranged in alphabetical order, the style for the citations vary. Among the most frequently used styles are the *American Psychological Association (APA)* and *Modern Language Association (MLA)*. The following information illustrates how to write source cards and bibliographies according to both the APA and MLA styles. First, there is the APA style for writing source cards and a bibliography written according to APA. Then, there are source cards that were written in MLA style and a bibliography written according to MLA.

APA Style for Recording a Book

```
Quinn, J. Bryant (1991). Making the most of
your money. New York: Simon & Schuster.
This book covers pragmatic and essential in-
formation about making and saving money. It
lists specific tips for cutting costs and
investing wisely. Chapter 6 provides excel-
lent coverage on understanding investments.
```

APA Style for Recording an Article in a Magazine

> Brenner, M. (1997, February). American nightmare: The
> ballad of Richard Jewell. Vanity Fair, 100–107, 150–159,
> 162–165.
> This article provides a sympathetic look at the life of
> Richard Jewell, formerly the FBI's prime suspect in the
> Oympic Park bombing. Jewell discusses his life as a
> national hero, his horrific experience with the media,
> and the accusations that he was responsible for bombing
> at the Olympics in Atlanta, Georgia, in 1996. The article
> focuses on personalities, providing numerous quotations
> from Jewell, his mother, his lawyers, and members of the
> FBI.

APA Style for Recording an Article in a Journal

> Rabouin, E.M. (1996). Revisioning business
> ethics. Women's Studies Quarterly, 24, 139–
> 145.
> This book discusses the integration of women's
> studies into a course not "naturally hospi-
> table or inclined to feminist integration."
> Provides a good theoretical base.

APA Style for Recording an Article in a Newspaper

> Uchitelle, L. (1997, February 16). Like oil and water: A tale of two economists. The New York Times, sec. 3 pp. 1, 5.
> This article compares the philosophies of two economic professors at Massachusettes Institute of Technology. Although Dr. Paul Krugman and Dr. Lester Thurow agree that income inequality and wage stagnation are big economic problems in the U.S., they disagree on the causes of and solutions to this situation.

APA Style for Recording a Videotape

> Janus Films (Producer). (1979). The role of women in the movies {Videotape}. Northbrook: Illinois: Coronet Films & Video.
> This videotape provides an overview of the roles of women throughout the 1920s, 1930s, and 1940s in film history.

With detailed information such as that provided on the preceding cards, you can easily write your bibliography. Examine the following bibliography written in an APA style. In this style, refer to your bibliography as "works cited," alphabetizing your sources according to the first letter in the citation. If the first word begins with *the, an,* or *a,* alphabetize according to the second word.

APA Bibliography

Works Cited

Brenner, M. (1997, February). American nightmare: The ballad of Richard Jewell. <u>Vanity Fair</u>, 100–107, 150–159, 162–165.

Janus Films (Producer). (1979). <u>The role of women in the movies</u> {Videotape}. Northbrook: Illinois: Coronet Films & Video.

Quinn, J. (1991). <u>Making the most of your money</u>. New York: Simon & Schuster.

Rabouin, E.M. (1996). Revisioning business ethics. <u>Women's Studies Quarterly, 24,</u> 139–145.

Uchitelle, L. (1997, February 16). Like oil and water: A tale of two economists. <u>The New York Times</u>, sec. 3 pp. 1, 5.

Now take a look at the MLA style for writing source cards and an MLA bibliography. First look at the source cards:

MLA Style for Recording a Book

Quinn, Jane Bryant. Making The Most of Your Money. New York: Simon & Schuster, 1991. This book covers pragmatic and essential information about making and saving money. It lists specific tips for cutting costs and investing wisely. Chapter 6 provides excellent coverage on understanding investing.

MLA Style for Recording an Article in a Monthly Magazine

Brenner, Marie. "American Nightmare: The Ballad of Richard Jewell." Vanity Fair February 1997: 100–107, 150–159, 162–165.
This article provides a sympathetic look at the life of Robert Jewell, at one time the FBI's prime suspect in the Olympic Park bombing. Jewell discusses his life. Good quotations from Jewell, attorneys, and the FBI.

MLA Style for Recording an Article in a Journal

Rabouin, E. Michelle. "Revisioning Business Ethics." Women's Studies Quarterly 24 (1996): 139–145.
Provides a good theoretical base for the integration of women's studies into a Business Ethics class.

MLA Style for Recording an Article in a Newspaper

> Uchitelle, Louis. "Like Oil and Water: A Tale of Two Economists." The New York Times 16 February 1997: Sec.3 page 1&5.
> This article compares the philosophies of two economic professors at Massachusettes Institute of Technology. Although Dr. Paul Krugman and Dr. Lester Thurow agree that income inequality and wage stagnation are big economic problems in the U.S., they disagree on the causes of and solutions to this situation.

MLA Style for Recording a Videotape

> The Role of Women in the Movies. Janus Films. Coronet Films & Video, 1979.
> Examines the stereotyping of women in movies and the influence of film roles on the behavior of the American public.

Make sure that you know what form your bibliography should take. Although the MLA and APA styles are frequently used, there are numerous other styles for your source cards and bibliography. The bibliography on the following page is written according to the MLA style. As you can see, there are some differences between The APA and MLA styles, but both forms list all the information that you need to find the original source.

MLA Bibliography

Bibliography

Brenner, Marie. "American Nightmare: The Ballad of
    of Richard Jewell." <u>Vanity Fair</u> February 1997:
    100-107, 150-159, 162-165.

Quinn, Jane Bryant. <u>Making the Most of Your Money</u>.
    New York: Simon & Schuster, 1991.

Raboun, E. Michelle "Revisioning Business Ethics."
    <u>Women's Studies Quarterly</u> 24 (1996): 139-145.

<u>The Role of Women in the Movies</u>. Janus Films.
    Coronet Films & Video.

Uchitelle, Louis. "Like Oil and Water: A Tale of
    Two Economists." <u>The New York Times</u> 16 February
    1997: sec. 3 page 1&5.

SUMMARY

This chapter focused on research and documentation. The chapter covered primary research, such as interviews and surveys, and secondary research, such as books, reference materials, periodicals, and the electronic media. The chapter also discussed documentation, focusing on the APA and MLA styles. Now that you're equipped with knowledge about research and documentation, it's time to turn your attention to Chapter 5, "Using Language."

Chapter Five

Using Language

Most of us take our language for granted. We grow up listening and speaking without much knowledge about or appreciation for the language we use. But we do need to respect our language, as it is directly connected to our human evolution. Ever since the first written symbols were recorded more than 5,000 years ago, language has been the basis of all human communication. Language has enabled humans to record ideas, to capture memories, and to share experiences with future generations. Language has been instrumental in advancing our civilization and elevating humankind above other animals.

One important aspect of language is that it is never stagnant. It is constantly changing to accommodate the society it serves. Language evolves as a result of internal forces such as the demands of citizens' groups and the addition of technological innovations. It also changes as a result of external forces such as war, international trading, and the immigration of refugees from other countries. When we read our Declaration of Independence, books authored by Emily Dickinson, or speeches given by Frederick Douglass, we realize the dramatic changes that have occurred in our language over the last 200 years. By recognizing the transformation of our language over its brief history, we will be more cognizant of and sensitive to the changes that will occur throughout our lifetimes.

Another fascinating characteristic of language is its arbitrary nature. The assignment of a certain word to an object or subject changes from country to country. We speak the language we do because our particular culture has assigned sounds and words to specific things and people. Whereas students from America label a *flower* as just that, Spanish students call it *flor*, the Chinese have assigned the word *hua* to mean the same thing, and in Hindi the word is *phool*. This arbitrary nature of language should remind you of the importance of being sensitive to foreign members of your audience. As a speaker, you can never think that your language is the only or superior language that is spoken.

This chapter focuses on the use of language in several important areas. You will examine how to make the language you use more interesting, understandable, and credible by taking a look at style, correct grammar, and cultural considerations in using language. Throughout this chapter, the emphasis is on selecting language that is most suitable for your audience, because the ultimate measure of success of speechmaking is the result you have on your audience.

STYLE

Mark Twain, nineteenth-century author of classics such as *Adventures of Huckleberry Finn* and *The Adventures of Tom Sawyer,* once said, "The difference between the almost right word and the right word is the difference between *lightning bug* and *lightning.*" Twain's quotation is as valid today as it was in the 1800s. It is important that you are knowledgeable about the impact of your selection of words and that your vocabulary reflects that knowledge. One area of language to consider is style. Style refers to the way in which something is said, expressed, or performed. In other words, style is the pattern of words and phrases you use in your speeches. There are many aspects of style, including the use of denotative and connotative language and forms of figurative speech.

Denotative and Connotative Meanings

Denotative meaning is what the word refers to in human experience. It is the shared objective interpretation that scholars rely on for definitions in dictionaries. Whereas denotative words are exact and literal, *connotative* words are more subjective in their meaning. Connotative words elicit associations and emotional overtones in an audience and are most effective in persuasive speeches. They rely on previous experiences and feelings that an audience may have. As you examine the following list of denotative and connotative words, think about the responses that you have to each word. Then, when you are composing your next speech, think about your selection of words and the response they will have on your audience.

Denotative Words	Connotative Words
untidy	slovenly
romance	love affair
slim	svelte
angry	livid
overweight	obese
unattractive	ugly
attractive	gorgeous
hungry	famished
tired	exhausted

Figurative Language

Another way to enhance the style of language you use is by incorporating figurative language into your speech. Figurative language is symbolic and a bit more ornate than nonfigurative speech. Compare the following examples of figurative and nonfigurative language:

Nonfigurative Language	Figurative Language
You are extremely important to me.	You are as important to me as food is to life.
I'm really tired.	I could sleep for a whole year.
It was scary.	Evil hovered over the town.
Please help our cause.	Think about the problem. Think about the solution. Think about helping.

There are several devices for creating figurative language. Some of the most frequently used techniques include similes, metaphors, personification, hyperbole, repetition, and alliteration.

A *simile* is a figure of speech that compares two essentially unlike things, often in a phrase introduced by *like* or *as*. "You're as sly as a fox," or "Being outside during a summer day in Phoenix, Arizona, is like being a foot away from a burning furnace," are examples of similes. *Metaphors,* on the other hand, are words or phrases that express a comparison as if the compared were part of a single phenomenon. "He's a sly fox," or "I've always considered you to be a workhorse," are examples of metaphors.

Personification is a figure of speech in which inanimate objects or abstractions are endowed with human qualities or are represented as possessing human form. "The raindrops danced on the roof," "The wind whistled through the trees," or "Life is a bowl of cherries," are examples of personification. Personification engages the audience by establishing a personal relationship with an object or abstraction.

Hyperbole is a figure of speech that uses exaggeration for emphasis or effect, as in, "This book weighs a ton," or "I could have danced all night." A speech writer once said that hyperbole "lies without deceiving."

Repetition can also be an extremely effective technique to use in your speech. By repeating a word, phrase, or sentence, you can reinforce an important thought. In Dr. Martin Luther King Jr.'s "I Have a Dream" speech, delivered in 1963, King was able to use repetition in an exemplary manner. He began eight consecutive sentences in the body of his speech with the words, "I have a dream." And in the conclusion of his speech, the words "let freedom ring" began ten out of the final thirteen sentences. Many speakers will repeat one sentence throughout an entire speech to emphasize one thought.

Alliteration refers to the repetition of the same letter or sound at the beginning of two or more consecutive words. Everyone, at one time or another, has probably recited the alliteration, "She sells seashells by the seashore." Although you might never use this saying in one of your speeches, you may want to use alliteration in another way. "Perseverance and persistence will pave the path to prosperity," could be an effective way to entice and interest your audience.

Through the use of similes, metaphors, personification, hyperbole, repetition, and alliteration, you can enhance the language you use in your speeches. And by improving your style, you will be creating a more complex and interesting speech.

CULTURAL CONSIDERATIONS

There are currently many individuals, groups, and federal agencies that advocate or demand equal treatment for all Americans. Every day we read and hear about prejudice and discrimination toward people because of color, sex, religion, ethnic origin and mental and physical abilities. As a speaker, you must be sensitive to the needs of all people. To make sure that you are treating all members of your audience in an egalitarian manner, you must use language that applies to everyone. This section examines nonsexist language and dialect, two areas of language that require awareness and sensitivity.

Nonsexist Language

Since the 1960s and the coinage of the word *sexist,* there have been vast changes toward a more gender-free language. Researchers, publishers, and activists of the feminist movement have made tremendous gains in recognizing the importance of an egalitarian language, and as a result, our ever-changing language is constantly being modified to accommodate social dictates. This section examines two important areas of nonsexist language where research and changes are occurring: first, it looks at characteristics of women's and men's speech, and second, it suggests guidelines for using nonsexist speech.

Research demonstrates that women's language is more polite, tactful, and diplomatic than men's. Women seem to be more concerned with interpersonal matters, whereas men are more concerned with factual communication and as a result, are more direct. It has frequently been stated that women seem more concerned with *rapport,* and men are more cued into the *report.* It has also been noted that women have a tendency to use more qualifiers, tag questions, and indirect speech than do men.

Qualifiers are words joined to another group of words that qualify or limit the meaning of the second group of words. Frequently used qualifiers include the following phrases:

- "I really don't know much about this subject, but . . ."
- "Although I'm really not an expert in this area, I'll . . ."
- "Because you probably know a great deal more about this than I . . ."

When a speaker uses qualifiers too much, audiences perceive the speaker to be ingratiating, lacking in esteem, and less influential. The bottom line, whether you are male or female, is to analyze your use of language and then, if you do use qualifiers excessively, decide if you want to change your speech patterns. The decision is yours. This same principle applies to all of the following discussions of language.

Women also use more tag questions in their language. A tag question is a question that appears after a statement, as if to verify the judgment. For example: "This is the most important case in the history of the judicial system, don't you agree?" This statement contains a tag question that may diminish the forcefulness of the statement. Generally, tag questions surface during the question and answer period, after a formal speech is delivered.

Indirectness in women's language is defined by excessive use of words such as "I feel" or "I guess" rather than "I think" at the beginning of sentences. In general, indirectness refers to the avoidance of clear and direct responses or statements. For example, rather than saying, "I'm chilly and we need to turn on the heat," an indirect response is, "Is it too cold in here for you?" Asking, "You wouldn't want to see the slide again, would you?" rather than asking, "Would you like to see the slide again?," is also an example of indirectness. Some authors state that women demonstrate more indirectness as a rule because they are more concerned with maintaining a positive relationship with an audience and, as a result, are inappropriately concerned about alienating the group. Certain feminists state that excessive indirectness is an indication of subordinate behavior and should be avoided when your role is to take command of the audience. In any case, be aware of your use of language and make the appropriate changes.

Research into men's language indicates that males are prone to interrupt someone with a statement, whereas women generally interrupt with questions. Although women are more likely to initiate conversations with a member of the opposite sex, men actually talk more than women. In research with mixed-sex dyads, small groups, and large presentations, men speak more than women, but they are less likely to maintain eye contact as long as women.

Although research supports the preceding generalizations, they are to be used as a tool to improve the language of both sexes. Each speaker should analyze his or her own use of language and then determine if changes are necessary. The goal is for both women and men to develop language that is neither subordinate nor threatening and to realize that the language we use influences how others see us as well as how we see ourselves.

Another cultural consideration focuses on words and terms that many women's groups, teachers' associations, and book publishers consider to be sexist and in need of change. Many people argue that change is necessary so that our language is inclusive of all humanity instead of half of the population. To avoid talk that may be insulting and offensive to one sex, try to incorporate these guidelines into your speech.

First, unless the person whom you are discussing is male, try to include both female and male pronouns into your speech. Take a look at the following examples that illustrate this point.

Instead of	Say
Each person will be pleased if he receives a present.	Each person will be pleased if he or she receives a present.
When everyone selects his present, we'll start the music.	When all the students select their presents, we'll start the music.
He might be curious about his fate.	One might be curious about one's fate.
As a student, he should read a lot.	As students, we should read a lot.

The National English Teachers Association, various publishing companies, and many parent-teacher associations issue guidelines for the use of nonsexist language. Their recommendations are made to correct any omissions of women or perpetuation of stereotypes. One area of criticism has focused on the use of *man*. Because the word *man* has come to refer almost exclusively to adult males, many groups endorse the following changes:

Instead of	*Say*
mankind	humanity
the best man for the job	best person
caveman	prehistoric people
common man	average person
chairman	chair, coordinator, chairperson
anchorman	anchor, reporter
fireman	firefighter
policeman	police officer
manmade	manufactured, artificial

Another area of nonsexist language focuses on the parallel treatment of men and women. This means that we need to use equivalent nouns to describe men and women, as in the following examples:

Instead of	*Say*
man and wife	husband and wife
men and girls	men and women
Chief Justice Rehnquist and Mrs. O'Connor	Chief Justice Rehnquist and Justice O'Connor
bachelor and spinster	single man and woman

It is also important to evaluate language to see if special forms are being used for one sex and not the other sex. Take a look at the following list of special forms and the suggested alternatives:

Instead of	Say
lady doctor	doctor, she
male nurse	nurse, he
airline stewardess	flight attendant

It is essential to remember that by incorporating these guidelines into your language, you will be treating both sexes in an egalitarian manner, delivering a speech that is nondiscriminatory and inclusive of all.

Ms.

Many people contend that there should be a parallel structure for using male and female titles. Because *Mr.* refers to both single and married males, *Ms.* (pronounced *mizz*) should be used for women. Unless a woman states a preference to be called Miss or Mrs., it's best to use the title *Ms.*

Dialect

Whether you are delivering or critiquing a speech, an important cultural consideration is the *dialect* of the audience or speaker. Dialect refers to a version of a standard language that differs in some aspects of grammar, vocabulary, or pronunciation. There are geographical and social dialects. Geographical dialects are divided into areas, such as New England, the Midwest, and the South. A New England dialect includes a pronunciation of *idea* as *idear*, whereas a Southern dialect includes the use of *y'all* for *you all*. Social dialects are developed by a particular group of people similar in education, social class, occupation, or ethnicity.

When you are communicating with an audience where members generally speak in a particular geographical or social dialect, preparation is particularly important. Although you should usually use standard English in your speeches, you need to be aware of the dialect your audience uses. You can always incorporate some aspect of the dialect into your speech, and you need to be able to understand any questions or comments that members of your audience may have.

COMMON ERRORS IN LANGUAGE

Have you ever listened to a speaker and known that something was wrong, but you weren't quite sure what it was? Perhaps what you were hearing was the incorrect use of language. Most people learn how to speak a language through imitation. We follow the rules of grammar that we hear and then pass them on through our own spoken words. Sometimes we inherit errors in the use of language and we may be totally unaware until they are brought to our attention. The problem is that these errors can lessen our credibility as a speaker, and so should be corrected. This section examines two frequent problems in the use of language: pointless words and phrases, and frequently misused words.

Pointless Words and Phrases

The following is a list of words and phrases that most audiences find annoying and irritating. Avoid them at all costs.

- . . . and so on and so forth
- . . . and all that that implies
- I'll have to save that information for another speech . . .
- I could discuss that topic for days . . .
- Sorry, I don't have time to explain this fully but . . .
- Before I begin my speech, I would like to say . . .
- I hope that I'm not boring you, but . . .
- To tell you the truth . . .

Frequently Misused Words

Can and May

The word *can* means "having the ability." The word *may* means "having the permission."

Wrong: Can I go to the library?

Right: May I go to the library?

Between and Among

Use *between* for two people, objects, or ideas. Use *among* when three or more are involved.

Wrong: The problem was discussed between Jim, Val, and Darrell.

Right: The problem was discussed among Jim, Val, and Darrell.

Affect and Effect

Affect is almost always a verb and *effect* is almost always a noun.

Wrong: The rain will effect us.

Right: The rain will affect us.

Wrong: I question the affect of this program.

Right: I question the effect of this program.

Farther and Further

Farther refers to a physical distance. You should use *further* in all other situations.

Wrong: How much further is Tucson?

Right: How much farther is Tucson?

Wrong: I will explain this farther next time.

Right: I will explain this further next time.

Irregardless and Regardless

Use only *regardless*. *Irregardless* is not a word.

Lay and Lie

Lay takes an object, whereas *lie* never does.

Wrong: Please lie these flowers on the table.

Right: Please lay these flowers on the table.

Wrong: If you're tired, lay down.

Right: If you're tired, lie down.

Different from and Different than

Use only different from; different than is incorrect.

Wrong: You are different than me.

Right: You are different from me.

Anyway and Anyways
Do not add an *s* to *anyway*, *nowhere*, or *somewhere*.

Doesn't and Don't
Wrong: He don't know anything about it.
Right: He doesn't know anything about it.

Always say:

I *don't*
You *don't*
We *don't*
They *don't*
He *doesn't*
She *doesn't*
It *doesn't*

Plenty
Note the exclusion of *plenty* in the following sentence.

Wrong: This is plenty cold.
Right: This is cold.

Slow and Slowly, Quick and Quickly
Most adverbs (parts of speech that modify verbs or adjectives) end in *ly*.

Wrong: You speak slow.
Right: You speak slowly.
Wrong: I ran quick.
Right: I ran quickly.

This Here and This
Wrong: This here is nice.
Right: This is nice.

Nothing and Anything
Wrong: I didn't know nothing about it.
Right: I didn't know anything about it.

Had Went and Had Gone
Wrong: We had went to school.
Right: We had gone to school.

More Nicer and Nicer, Most Nicest and Nicest

Adjectives (parts of speech that modify nouns and pronouns) express degrees of comparison if you add *er* (used with two items) or *est* (used with three or more items). You can also indicate degrees of comparison by adding *more* and *most* in front of the object or subject that is being modified. Do not use both means of comparison.

Wrong: She is the more nicer of the two girls.

Right: She is the nicer of the two girls.

Wrong: He is the most healthiest person alive.

Right: He is the healthiest person alive.

He is the most healthy person.

Her and Her Mother and She and Her Mother, Him and Me and He and I

Personal pronouns that are used as subjects include *I, we, you, he, she,* and *they. Her* is a personal pronoun used in the ojective and possessive cases. *Him* and *me* are personal pronouns used in the objective case. Try each pronoun separately to see whether it sounds right. This will help you when stating combinations like the following:

Wrong: Her and her mother went to the library.

Right: She and her mother went to the library.

Wrong: Him and me are going home.

Right: He and I are going home.

Hanged and Hung

Hang, hanged, and *hanged* refer to executions or suicides whereas *hang, hung,* and *hung* refer to objects.

Wrong: She hung herself rather than spend her life addicted to heroin.

Right: She hanged herself rather than spend her life addicted to heroin.

Saw and Seen

Wrong: I seen it.

Right: I saw it or I have seen it.

Done and Did

Wrong: I done it.

Right: I did it or I have done it.

Being aware of these frequently made errors will assist you in perfecting your use of language and ultimately increase your credibility with your audience.

SUMMARY

This chapter on language has examined style, nonsexist language, and frequently made errors. The chapter also noted that, as a speaker, you must stay aware of contemporary changes in language as well as traditional rules of grammar. A good grasp of language can only make you a more credible and interesting speaker.

Chapter Six

Delivering Your Speech

Lawrence Winfrey was ready. He had spent more than thirty hours researching, writing, and rehearsing his speech about the negative effects of taking synthetic steroids to increase muscle mass and enhance strength. Lawrence had shown his speech outline to family and friends and had received favorable responses from everyone. He had talked about his topic with his teacher, and she seemed impressed. And besides, Lawrence was speaking on a topic that he knew well. Lawrence had taken steroids for four years while he wrestled in high school, and he had experienced the dreadful consequences of the drug. Now he was going to share with his class his experiences and his impassioned opinion of using steroids. Lawrence was speaking on a topic he knew, had researched fully, and felt strongly about. What more could his audience want?

About one minute into his speech, Lawrence caught a glimpse of one of his classmates whose head bobbed down as he drifted off to sleep. Two minutes into his speech, Lawrence heard some people in the back of the room whispering, and by the time he concluded his talk, it seemed that no one was listening to him except his teacher. And she was evaluating him and had to pay attention.

Lawrence was stunned, disappointed, and resigned to the fact that he was a failure at public speaking. Then later he met with his speech teacher and viewed a videotape of his speech. Immediately Lawrence realized that even though the content of his speech was brilliant, there was definitely a problem with his delivery. During his speech, Lawrence had stared at his notes, avoiding eye contact with his audience, his posture was slouched, and his hands were glued to the lectern. His voice was barely audible. It took only a few minutes for Lawrence to make the judgment that he looked bored and that he needed to concentrate on more effective eye contact, posture, and verbal delivery.

Like Lawrence, many speakers are so concerned with *what* they are to say that they are unaware of *how* they say it. Although a speech must be well researched, clearly organized, and based on strong evidence, it also needs to be presented effectively. Researchers have found that body language and verbal delivery have a tremendous impact on an audience. Research has also demonstrated that your voice and physical movement can win over an audience, even if the content is weak.

Audiences are consciously and unconsciously responding to a speaker's voice, gestures, posture, stance, and eye contact. The bottom line in public speaking and, in fact, in all communication, is that, as a scholar once stated, "One cannot *not* communicate." In other words, you are always relating something to your audience. The key is to make sure that your delivery enhances, emphasizes, and reinforces the message you are trying to convey.

One of the most important principles in public speaking is that your delivery needs to be natural. You want your audience to be able to relate to you, and you accomplish this by displaying enthusiasm, anger, or whatever emotion your material commands. Deliver your speech as though you are conversing with individuals in the audience and not reading a written text. As Quintilian, a Roman scholar and orator of the first century, so aptly stated, "He who speaks as though he were reciting forgets the whole charm of what he has written."

This chapter focuses on the elements involved in an effective delivery. You will examine the nonverbal and verbal components involved in presenting your speech. You will also look at some external factors that are important in speechmaking. Throughout this chapter, the emphasis is on how you can deliver your well-constructed text in a manner that will reach and positively affect your audience. After all, this is important because it's *what your audience gets* that really counts.

NONVERBAL DELIVERY

For centuries, politicians and great orators have been aware of the influence of delivery on an audience. Winston Churchill, Ronald Reagan, Jimmy Carter, and John F. Kennedy all worked with speech consultants to perfect their deliveries and influence the masses. Today, speech coaches assist professors, salespeople, and CEOs of corporations to improve their skills.

The easiest delivery skills to critique and improve are the nonverbal techniques. These skills are those that people can see but not hear, such as eye contact, posture and stance, gestures and movement, facial expression, and dress.

Eye Contact

Eye contact can help a speaker in two important ways. First, by using a constant yet natural eye gaze, a speaker can engage audience members by convincing them that the message is just for them. There is nothing more desirable than having individuals in your audience think that you are talking to them alone. Eye contact can assist you in your quest to accomplish this goal.

You can achieve effective eye contact by looking directly at the individuals in your audience instead of staring at the wall, the ceiling, or your outline. Look at individuals in different sections of the room and develop eye contact with someone in the front of the room. Then look at someone in the middle of the room, followed with eye contact with another person on the left side. Rotate your contact in a natural manner, and make sure that you circulate throughout the room. It's important to talk to these people by looking directly into their eyes. Try not to tune in to only the people who are nodding in agreement or those who are diligently taking notes. Involve your whole audience. As is the case in interpersonal and small group communication, you need to include everyone who is there to hear you. Avoidance of certain people may lead to disinterested, if not alienated, members of your audience. It's also important that you keep your eyes on the audience, glancing occasionally at your notes, and not be distracted by the jogger outside, the painting on the wall, or the fly on the ceiling. Chances are great that if you stare excessively at some object or person, so will your audience. Remember that effective eye contact with your audience will help to establish a personal relationship with them, and nothing could be better than that.

The second reason that eye contact is important is because it enables a speaker to gauge how he or she is doing. A speaker can see the quizzical expression of someone who needs additional explanation or the broad smile of half a dozen people who appreciate your sense of humor. Looking at an audience gives a speaker the immediate feedback needed.

Posture and Stance

As a child, were you ever told to "stand up straight and tall"? If you were, join the club of millions of other children who were told the same thing. If you weren't reminded to stand erect, congratulations on your fine posture. In either case, when you speak to a group, you'll need to stand with shoulders back, chest up, and stomach tucked in. It's also important to place your feet shoulder width apart with an equal distribution of weight on both feet. Research has shown that an erect posture conveys confidence, in addition to creating a physical environment for the production of a fuller voice. Remember not to assume a rigid posture (unless you're in the military or in a back brace) and never lean too much on one foot. By being aware of good posture and stance, you can incorporate these skills into a natural delivery.

Gestures and Movement

Gestures are motions of the limbs or body that express or help to express thought. They can emphasize or reinforce an idea or opinion. Imagine a speech without a shrug of the shoulders, a pointed finger in the air, or hands placed together as if in prayer. Gestures add a great deal to a speech. They add interest and expression and help to keep the attention of an audience. The most important aspect about using gestures is that they need to be natural and sincere. Audiences can sense when the pounding fist on the lectern or a clenched fist is contrived and unnatural. When a speaker is relaxed and thoroughly absorbed in the material, gestures will naturally reinforce and emphasize an important point.

Some speakers find it easy to coordinate their fingers to the number of the point they're making. Most people, when describing the size of something or someone, will use gestures in space. Demonstrations on woodworking, painting, gardening, and the like are perfect vehicles to use your hands. In whatever type of speech you are giving, it's important to remember that unless gestures appear natural, they just don't work.

Some people find it impossible to express themselves with their hands during a speech. The best advice in this situation is to lightly hold on to the lectern or position your hands on top of the podium. Then, with each new speech, add a gesture or two until this nonverbal technique becomes a part of your presentations.

There are definitely some things that you never want to do during a speech. These include twisting your hair, scratching your head, or rubbing your jewelry. It's also best to keep your hands out of your pockets and never take anything to the podium except your speech outline, a glass of water, and visual aids. Too many speakers distract their audiences by popping the lids off of magic markers, hitting the lectern with a pen, and playing with a paper clip or rubber band. If a speaker attends to an object, so will the audience.

If you're speaking to an international audience, make sure that you're aware of the use and meaning of gestures in a particular culture. Like language, gestures and their meanings vary from country to country. The thumb and forefinger in a circle gesture that means, "Everything is great" to Americans, would mean, "You're worth nothing," to the French and perhaps something worse to other nationalities. Even a simple vertical movement of the head may mean, "Yes" to Americans, whereas Greeks or Turks see this gesture as meaning, "No." A little research before delivering a speech can prevent you from giving mixed messages or offending a foreign audience.

Movement, whether it is a twist of the head or steps from the lectern, call attention to the speaker and the speech. Make sure that you coordinate what you say with what you do. Movement can be particularly effective when you can break down the artificial barrier that the lectern creates between you and your audience. With smaller groups, walking toward the audience can help to create a personal relationship. If you're using a microphone at the lectern or you're being videotaped, whole body movement may be impossible. When it's impossible to move from the podium, you might bend slightly forward from the waist to emphasize an important point. Incorporating natural gestures and movement into your nonverbal delivery will result in a more attentive audience.

Facial Expression

There are two important words that indicate what you should do with your face when you are speaking: Be natural. Let your subject matter dictate your expression. When you discuss starvation in Third World countries, a serious expression is appropriate. During a speech on the funniest comedian in the world, experience the subject matter. Just remember that everyone appreciates a pleasant expression before and after the speech—and during, if it is appropriate.

Dress

A recent Roper Organization public opinion poll asked men and women what they noticed first in people of the same sex and the opposite sex. Somewhat surprisingly, women first noticed what people of both sexes were wearing. Men first noticed a woman's build and a man's clothing. What the results of this poll suggest is that what you wear does make a difference to your audience. The best advice about what to wear is that you should appear clean, neat, comfortable, and appropriate for the situation. Looking as good as you can is always a confidence builder, and ultimately your audience will place more faith in what you say.

Tips for Nonverbal Delivery

1. Develop eye contact with individuals in all parts of the audience. Make people feel as if you are talking to them alone.

2. Use natural hand gestures that accentuate your speech, not distract from it.

3. Dress appropriately and comfortably.

4. Know what your gestures will mean to foreign members of your audience.

5. All of your body language is interdependent. Relax, be natural, and your personal style will emerge.

VERBAL DELIVERY

When asked to describe their voice, most people are quite certain about what they like or dislike. Statements such as, "I sound like a child," "People think my voice is sexy," or, "No one ever understands my accent," are characteristic. Surprisingly, approximately one-third of all Americans state that they would change their voice if they could. Although 67 percent of us are in luck, there's hope for the rest who are not satisfied with their voice, because they can change the way they sound. There are several components of a voice that people can alter to achieve a more pleasing verbal image. The major factors include volume, rate, and pitch. Other aspects include pronunciation and enunciation. This section examines each of these factors, beginning with volume.

Volume

The most easily identifiable aspect of your voice is the volume. If you're not audible to everyone in the room, then you're not fulfilling your job as a speaker. On the other hand, if you speak too loudly, then your audience will be begging for a reprieve. To know how loud you need to be, and whether or not you need a microphone, find out how large your room is and how many people will fill that space. If possible, rehearse your speech in the actual room or a replica of that space.

Although the rule of thumb is to speak loudly enough for everyone to hear, it's also important to vary the volume of your voice depending on what you say. Notice how professional speakers alternate the volume of their voices. When discussing a secret or private encounter, a whisper can be most appropriate, whereas, when speaking about challenge and victory, raising the volume of your voice works. Just remember that, as in life, variety is the spice.

Rate

Rate, or the number of words you speak in any given unit of time, is another important part of your voice. Most Americans speak an average of 115 words per minute, and most people can process far more words than that. If you deliver a speech too quickly (usually because of nervousness), you might slur your words and otherwise articulate poorly, sending your audience into a frenzy. A speech spoken too slowly will either result in a frustrated audience or one that has been lulled to sleep. The key is to vary the rate of your words. During an exciting section of your speech, speed up the delivery, and when you tell a sentimental tale, slow down. You can achieve rhythm by changing tempos over part of or your entire speech. Just remember that a change of pace is your goal.

If you speak with a strong accent or dialect, then *slow* may be the only way to go. You want everyone to understand you; if experience has demonstrated that the only way this is possible is by slowing down, then by all means do so. It's far better to speak slowly than to speed through and have no one understand what you have said.

Another dynamic aspect of rate is the use of pauses. By pausing between words, phrases, or sentences, you can emphasize what came before or after the silence. Suppose that in a speech on drug abuse you include a rhetorical question such as, "Have you, or any member of your family, ever experienced a dependence so strong that the most important thing in life was that dependence?" A few seconds of silence after this rhetorical question gives the audience a few moments to consider the cognitive and emotional aspects of what you are asking. Pauses punctuate your thoughts, prevent you from speaking too quickly, and add a dramatic effect unachievable any other way. The ultimate result is an attentive audience, caught in your web of effective vocal delivery.

Pitch

Pitch is the high or low notes you produce. People speak with a range of approximately eight notes; with training, most people can increase their range. A voice that is very high is considered childlike, and a voice that is very low is generally considered sexy. We raise the pitch of our voice at the end of a question and lower it at the end of a statement. If you speak at one pitch throughout your speech, you'll be accused of being monotone, or worse yet, boring. Your ultimate goal is to speak in a low, calm voice, incorporating small shifts in pitch.

The tone of your voice is created by resonance, or the vibrating quality. Tone refers to the richness of your voice and is created when the air you exhale vibrates against the surfaces within your chest and nasal cavity. You can have a nasal, thin, scratchy, or rich voice, depending on the amount of vibration that occurs. To achieve a richer tone, on exhalation, push the air against your throat, head, and particularly the bridge of your nose.

People who sound nasal may be taught to slow down their rate of speech and open their mouths more to give the air a better chance of coming out of their mouth instead of their nose. Anyone who is motivated and willing to concentrate and practice can change the tone of voice.

Nonfluencies

There comes a time in everyone's life when they are at a loss for words. Perhaps a person is excited or nervous or just plain unprepared to speak. Whatever the reason, there is a tendency for people to fill up the silence with nonfluencies (also known as vocalized pauses and space fillers) such as, "uh," "er," "ah," "um," "like," or "y'know." Some speakers begin each sentence with a nonfluency. After a while, audience members may begin to count how many times the speaker says "uh" or "um." Consequently, what started as an innocent space filler becomes a major distraction. The best advice is to eliminate nonfluencies from your speech and settle for a moment of silence instead. By viewing a videotape of your speech, you can determine whether you need to work on eliminating nonfluencies.

Some people also stutter or stumble over words when they're excited or stressed. The best thing to do in this situation is to pause, pull yourself together, and begin again. You can always apologize if you feel so inclined, but try not to make a big deal out of an innocent mistake. Never obsess about stuttering or stumbling over words, as your audience will quickly forget and forgive.

Pronunciation and Enunciation

A thesaurus and a dictionary are two friends that a speaker should never be without. A thesaurus is a wonderful reference book for looking up synonyms (words that mean the same thing), and a dictionary will provide you with not only definitions, but also the accepted pronunciation of a word. The pronunciation is placed in parentheses and written phonetically. If you're having problems with the phonetic code, a phonetic guide is always written in the beginning of your dictionary. If your dictionary lists two or more pronunciations, the first phonetic spelling is the preferred one.

It is of the utmost importance to pronounce correctly all the words you use. Mispronunciation of any difficult, foreign, or technical word can damage your credibility. You may want to record the phonetic spelling of unfamiliar words on your outline or notecard. If an extremely important name or place is spelled differently than it sounds, consider writing that word on the board or on a large visual aid for your audience. Under no circumstance is it acceptable to say, "I don't know how to pronounce this," or "Does anyone know the correct pronunciation of this word?" As the speaker, you are responsible for finding out this information before you stand in front of the group.

Over the last ten years, a group of college instructors has accumulated a list of some of the most common errors in pronunciation. Take a look at the following list and see if you need to correct your pronunciation of any of these words. The mispronunciation and accepted pronunciation lists are written as they sound.

Word/Name	Mispronunciation	Accepted Pronunciation
library	li-*bare*-e	*li*-brar-e
pen	*pin*	*pen*
get	*git*	*get*
ask	*axe*	*ask*
clique	*click*	*cleek*
theater	thee-*ate*-er	*thee*-a-ter
legislator	leg-is-la-*tor*	*leg*-is-la-ter
police	*po*-lees	po-*lees*
mischievous	mis-*chee*-vee-us	*mis*-cha-vus
genuine	*jen*-you-wine	*jen*-you-un

often	*off*-ten	*off*-en
picture	*pitch*-er	*pik*-tur
subtle	*sub*-tul	*sut*-tl
route	*rout*	*root*
Iowa	*I*-o-way	*I*-o-wuh

Enunciation is the distinctness and clarity of the sound, involving clear articulation of each syllable of a word. Both enunciation and pronunciation occur when your lips, teeth, tongue, and soft palate come in contact in various positions. Problems in both enunciation and pronunciation arise when one or more of the components are in incorrect placement. Common enunciation errors include leaving off the final *g* in a word like *going*, to running words together as in *Gonnagodamovie?*

The following list contains examples of common enunciation errors:

Instead of	*Say*
dancin'	dancing
gonna	going
whatcha doin'?	what are you doing?
meetcha at the store	meet you at the store
Febuary	February
dat fadda	that father
ta go	to go
da Bronx	the Bronx

Mumbling is a common enunciation problem that is caused by partially closing the mouth and lowering the pitch of your voice. The cure for mumbling is to open the mouth, raise the pitch, and move your lips. It's often been said that a lip reader finds it almost impossible to decipher the words of a mumbler, so speak with lively lips, clearly enunciating each syllable of a word.

Improper pronunciation and indistinct enunciation can ruin the verbal delivery of a speech. Keep a dictionary on hand when you are preparing your speech, practice self-evaluation of your verbal skills, and videotape or audiotape your speech to evaluate the clarity of your talk.

Tips for Verbal Delivery

1. Vary the volume and rate of your speech. Variety adds spice to your speech.

2. Use pauses for dramatic effect.

3. Use inflection to enhance your verbal delivery.

4. Pause instead of using a nonfluency.

5. Use a dictionary to clarify pronunciations. Keep a phonetic record of difficult, foreign, and technical words so that you know how to pronounce them.

6. Enunciate clearly to increase your credibility.

EXTERNAL FACTORS

Occasionally a speaker must deal with problems that arise inside or outside of the area where a speech is being delivered. Suppose that you're delivering a speech on the rising cost of health care, and suddenly an ambulance siren drowns out your voice. Or your audience keeps standing because the seats are too hard or, worse yet, someone trips exiting from the dark area where you're speaking. These are all examples of external conditions that interfere with your speech. External conditions include seating, lighting, sound, amplification of your voice, and any factor that hinders the presentation of your speech. Often a speaker is so absorbed in writing and rehearsing a speech that he or she forgets to examine the environment where the speaker is to deliver the speech. The following guidelines will help you to make sure the space where you're speaking is conducive to delivering and receiving a message.

First, make sure there is the right amount of space for your audience. Although this may sound simple enough, there have been many speeches delivered to a group of 50 sweaty people packed into a room with a seating capacity of 20. On the other hand, if your audience numbers 20, and you have a room that accommodates 200, you may spend all of your time walking around the room to relate to your audience. A room that is too large for a group also makes the audience feel unconnected. To create a conducive atmosphere for sending and receiving your message, make sure the size of your room is suitable for your audience. Suitability also involves having desk space for your audience if they need to write and checking out the comfort of the chairs if your audience will be sitting for a long time.

Second, make sure there is sufficient light for both you and your audience. If people are to take notes, and you need to use your outline, then check on the lighting.

And if you ever have the opportunity to speak before a large crowd and you're lit with a spotlight, then make sure your audience has enough light to move in and out of the auditorium.

Third, you may run into a situation where sound is drowning out your speech. Suppose that you're delivering a speech and someone starts yelling in the hall. Wait until the distraction is over. The same rule applies if a dog is barking outside or a television is blaring in the next room. If the disturbance doesn't stop, and if you can be heard by talking louder, do so. In certain situations, you may have to stop your speech by stating, "Excuse me while I attend to this matter," and physically do something about the television or the dog.

Perhaps you're giving a speech and someone walks in late or makes a lot of noise in the back of the room. Again, wait until the distraction ceases and then begin where you left off. If a stare doesn't quiet someone down, you may have to request that the person be quiet. You are in charge, if only for a few minutes, and it is up to you to handle any disruption.

Fourth, when you speak to groups of more than 200 people, you need to use a microphone. Again, preparation pays off. Make sure that the amplification equipment works and that you know how to work it. Don't let screeching feedback from a microphone interfere with your talk. Leave about six to eight inches between your mouth and a standard microphone, and if you plan to move around, wear a lavalier microphone. They're small, clip on, and enable you to come in closer contact with your audience. Also, always know where you'll stand, then move around and set your outline. Don't wait until you are ready to speak to find out the podium you had planned to use is nonexistent. The bottom line with external factors is that you are responsible for making sure that the environment in which you speak is conducive to delivering and receiving your message.

SUMMARY

In this chapter, you have focused on nonverbal and verbal delivery skills. The nonverbal delivery skills you have examined include eye contact, posture and stance, gestures and movement, facial expression, and dress. Verbal delivery skills include volume, rate, pitch, the elimination of nonfluencies, pronunciation, and enunciation. The chapter also discussed external factors. By perfecting your delivery skills, you will become a dynamic public speaker.

Chapter Seven

Using Visual Aids

In a speech on the dangerous effects of smoking, Cassy was able to cite study after study that demonstrated the correlation between smoking and numerous diseases. She was also able to quote the Surgeon General and multiple other experts who stated the harmful effects of both primary and secondary cigarette smoke. Then, to emphasize her point further, Cassy showed her audience two X-rays: one of a smoker's lungs, and the other of lungs of someone who had never smoked. Her audience was aghast when looking at the black lungs of the smoker and the clear lungs of the nonsmoker. Cassy had made her point.

Like Cassy, you'll find visual aids—materials that assist you in making or supporting main points in your speech—may be some of the most convincing evidence that you can use. Visual aids are extremely important, because they can make the information in your speech more clear, interesting, and dramatic.

This chapter focuses on the functions and types of visual aids. It discusses the pros and cons of using three-dimensional aids, posters, flip charts, overhead transparencies, slides, and videotapes in your speeches, as well as listing some important tips to follow when incorporating visual aids into your speech.

FUNCTIONS OF VISUAL AIDS

Although you alone are the primary medium for the delivery of information in your speeches, you can also use visual aids most effectively to clarify, reinforce, or emphasize a point you are making. Visual aids help an audience comprehend and retain information and stay interested in your material. In addition, visual aids can help to ease the anxiety of standing in front of an audience. The audience's gaze switches from the speaker to the visual aid, and this in itself can relieve a great deal of tension.

It has been documented innumerable times that visual aids increase the comprehension of your speech. Instead of spending 15 minutes in a complex explanation of the basics of using a computer program, why not set up a computer and demonstrate how to use it? Rather than describing the beauty of the Grand

Canyon, begin or end your talk with slides of the canyon. If the specific purpose of your speech is to inform your audience about how to make enchiladas, then show a transparency of the ingredients and make them in front of the class. An enlarged photograph of war-torn Beirut or Sarajevo would be worth a thousand words of explanation. Often a single visual aid can relate in a few seconds what otherwise may take minutes to explain.

Visual aids can also improve audience retention of information. Studies indicate that three days after a speech without visual aids, an audience will recall, at the very most, 25 percent of what was said. However, when visual aids are incorporated into a speech, the retention rate after three days increases dramatically. If you're like most people, how many times have you attended a lengthy lecture only to remember clearly the visual aids? The bottom line is that research and personal experience clearly demonstrate the importance of using visual aids.

Among the most frequently used visual aids are three-dimensional aids, posters, flip charts, overhead transparencies, slides, videotapes, and handouts. Many professional speakers use two or more of these visual aids during a speech. Although using more than one visual aid can add variety and keep the attention of your audience, more is not always better. Always consider whether or not a visual aid will help to explain or reinforce an idea, and remember that visual aids serve the purpose of enhancing, not replacing, what you say. If you decide to use a visual aid, ask yourself if it is clear, simple, and necessary. If you can answer yes to these questions, you're in business.

THREE-DIMENSIONAL AIDS

Three-dimensional aids are materials that have length, width, and depth. You can effectively incorporate both animate beings and inanimate objects into your speech. If you're delivering a speech on the correct way to administer a Piaget test to a toddler, it would be imperative that you bring in the objects that are used in testing and, depending on time restraints, you could even administer one test to a child. When you're demonstrating the steps involved in creating a Native American dream catcher, bring in dream catchers in various stages of creation. For a speech on the importance of recycling, what could be more dramatic than bringing in 28 pounds of trash, the average amount of trash American families throw away each week? How effective would a speech on the most effective way to tee off be without a golf ball and golf club? Three-dimensional visual aids can be a simple yet most effectual way to complement your speech.

POSTERS

Posters are large visual aids printed on paper that generally contain simple lines, bold colors, and a minimum amount of lettering. They relate information quickly and are always visible at a distance. Although decorative posters are printed on light-weight paper, it's best to use stiff and sturdy poster paper for your visual aids. You'll find it is much easier to handle and position a stronger poster, and there's less chance they'll tear.

Some types of illustrations frequently seen on posters include drawings, charts, and graphs. Some types of drawings that work well as posters include maps, architectural blueprints, and micro and macro representations of animate beings and inanimate objects. If you're an artist, you can make your own drawings. If not, most libraries and print shops have machines that enlarge any drawing from a book. Just make sure that you use bold lines and colors that the audience can see from the back of the room, and, on each two-dimensional aid, place a heading that clearly spells out to your audience what it is.

Charts are another type of illustration frequently depicted on posters. Charts are visual aids with only words on a page, such as a list of ingredients for a recipe, key words in an outline, or steps in a procedure. Audiences are more likely to remember simple information, so never exceed ten words or five lines on a chart and avoid using complete sentences. When preparing any visual aid, don't overload your audience with too much information on one sheet, and always ask yourself if your audience will be able to grasp the visual aid's content.

Graphs, another type of illustration that you can draw on posters, are figures that show the relationships among quantities. Most audiences seem to comprehend data much better when it is represented in a bar graph, line graph, or circle graph.

Bar graphs consist of vertical or horizontal bars that show comparisons. Statistical information is written on the grids (usually to the left and bottom of the graph) with a maximum of 10 bars per graph.

Line graphs consist of lines plotted on x and y axes. They are excellent visual aids to use when you want to illustrate an increase, decrease, growth, or decline over a period of time. As in bar graphs, a line graph displays statistical information to the left and bottom of the graph.

A circle graph represents 100 percent of the subject, with sections (shaped like pie slices) proportional to the percent they represent. You've probably seen the national budget illustrated by a circle graph. Such graphs are the ideal visual aid when you need to illustrate the relationship of various parts to the whole.

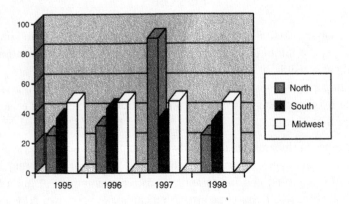

FLIP CHARTS AND BOARDS

Flip charts can be quite effective when you are speaking to a group of 40 or less. They're relatively easy to make, informal, and economical. The major drawback is that you sacrifice eye contact when you write on the chart. To shorten the time your back is toward your audience, write one or just a few words at a time on the chart during your speech or prepare part of your information before your speech. A general rule of thumb is to equate 1 inch of lettering for every 15 feet of distance from the visual aid. So, if the farthest person from your flip chart is 15 feet away, then 1-inch-high letters should be fine. If your farthest person is 30 feet away, then use 2-inch-high letters. Although this rule generally works, it's always a good idea to sit in the back of the room to get the right proportions of letters, and to find out the elevation necessary for the flip chart to be visible. If people can't see your visual aid, then it's not helping you.

Like flip charts, chalkboards and white boards that use felt-tipped pens are inexpensive to use and easy to write on. The negative aspects of using them are that they can be messy (have you ever tried to wipe chalk off your back?) and require that you turn your back to your audience. Unfortunately, it's not a great idea to write all of your information on the board before your speech, as your audience will be attending to future information rather than staying with you.

OVERHEAD TRANSPARENCIES

Overhead transparencies have two advantages over flip charts and boards. First, you don't have to turn your back to your audience, and second, they are relatively easy to make and you can use them with a much larger group. Most people think overhead transparencies look more professional and consequently increase your credibility as a speaker. If you don't have the capability of making transparencies on a computer, most print shops and many libraries can print them for you.

When you use a transparency, rehearse the speech with an overhead projector. As is the case with all visual aids, know when and how long you'll be showing your aid. The average person can comprehend approximately twenty words in 10 seconds, and most people tire of a drawing after about 30 seconds. Turn on the projector when you're using your transparency, and make sure that you turn it off when you're not using it. There's nothing worse than trying to talk or listen over the sound of a noisy projector, or facing the projector's blinding light in the front of the room. Also, when you use a transparency, point to the screen and not the transparency itself so you won't block any audience member's view of the image.

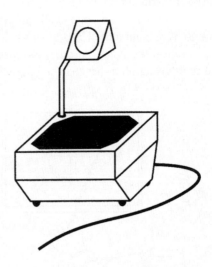

PHOTOGRAPHS AND SLIDES

As you've heard many times, a picture is worth a thousand words, so photographs can minimize the amount of talking you need to do to explain a point. Photographs can be incredibly effective when you're persuading someone to travel to a scenic location, showing the results of surgery with pre- and postsurgery shots, or trying to stir up emotion in your audience. Just watch people's reaction when shown a picture of a cuddly puppy, a starving baby, or a homeless senior citizen.

The most important thing about using photographs is to make sure they are large enough. When speaking to a small group of approximately 25 people, make sure your photograph is at least 11 by 14 inches. Or you may want to consider making your print into an overhead transparency or slide. It's never a good idea to pass around your standard-size photographs during your speech because the audience's attention will shift to that aid and to the process of passing it on to another person. If you absolutely must pass your photograph or another visual aid around the room, do so after you are finished speaking and only if there's time to do so.

If you are speaking to a large group, you may want to consider showing slides. Slides of your favorite paradise are an engaging way to begin or end a travel speech, and speeches about athletics, dance, or the fine arts are perfect subjects for slides. The major problems with using slides are that you need to show them in the dark, at the cost of making eye contact, and you need to contend with technology that may not work. However, if you make sure to place all of your slides correctly in a carousel, you have an extra bulb handy, you have a slide projector that enables you to stand in front of the group, and you have rehearsed with your equipment, then nothing could be better than slides. Also, make sure the focus is working properly and that you turn off the projector when you are not using it.

VIDEOTAPE

A videotape recording of your parachute jump will undoubtedly increase your audience's enjoyment of an entertaining speech on your latest hobby. A videotape of a cocaine user who ruined her life as a result of her drug addiction will probably do more to persuade your audience to "just say no" than almost any other form of evidence. What could be more educational about birthing than a videotape of the birthing process? In essence, a videotape can play an important role in making your speech more interesting, clear, and easy to remember.

There are several considerations when using videotapes in your speeches. First, you must make sure everyone in the room can see your visual aid. Many people say that the distance between the audience and the video monitor should be no more than five times the width of the monitor. It's a good idea to take a back seat and conduct a sight test before your speech. Second, decide when and how you'll use the tape. Will it be used in the beginning, at the end, or at a major point during your speech? Will you use sound from the videotape or will you narrate? Third, make sure that you know all there is to know about the equipment. For instance, do you know how to turn the recorder on and off without generating any static? Is your tape recorded at the proper speed for the videorecorder you're using? Finally, and most importantly, you must decide on a plan of action to deliver your speech without this visual aid if your videotape or equipment malfunctions. What will you do if your tape breaks or if the extension cord doesn't reach the electrical socket? Videotapes and any visual aid that require equipment can be exciting to use if everything goes as you plan, but it can be a nightmare if something goes wrong. So plan ahead and rehearse, rehearse, rehearse!

HANDOUTS

There are four important things to remember about using handouts. First, make sure they're legible. There's nothing worse than receiving a handout that is only partially legible because of light print or a half-copied page. Second, make sure you've included an article or document in its entirety. You can alienate your audience by including a page with "continued" written at the bottom of a sheet and then neglecting to include the continued section. Third, if you're handing out a copied article, include a complete citation on the first page. Finally, it's best to wait until your speech is over to distribute your handouts. If you hand them out any earlier, people will focus on them rather than you.

Tips for Using Visual Aids

1. Be sure that your visual aid is necessary. Ask yourself whether the aid will help to explain, reinforce, or highlight your point.

2. Your visual aids need to be simple, clear, and legible. If people can't see or understand them, there's no point in using them.

3. Show your audience where to look when using your aid. A pointer will help you to accomplish that goal.

4. Always address your audience rather than your visual aid. Turn your back to the audience only if necessary and only for short periods of time.

5. Proofread all of your information. A misspelled word or incorrect statistic can damage your credibility.

6. Display only one visual aid at a time. Don't overload your audience with your aids.

7. Exhibit your visual aid when you'll be using it, then put it away.

8. Label and explain your visual aid. Never take for granted that your audience knows what you haven't told them.

9. Rehearse using your visual aid in your speech. Know when and how to use your aids and any equipment. It's also a good idea to write on your speech outline when you'll be using your aid.

10. Be prepared! Decide what you'll do if your equipment doesn't work or your handouts don't arrive back from the printer in time for your speech. Preparation for your speech can save you a great deal of anguish.

SUMMARY

This chapter discussed how visual aids can clarify, enhance, and reinforce ideas that you make in your speech. It also examined various types of aids and listed some pragmatic tips for their use. By incorporating visual aids into your speeches, you'll find that your audience will better understand the message you are trying to convey. And as you know, this is the ultimate goal of public speaking.

Chapter Eight

Listening, Evaluating, and Perfecting

Most people spend approximately 80 percent of their waking hours in situations like school, work, or social interactions where listening is the paramount skill. In addition, every day we are bombarded with audio messages from radio, acquaintances, friends, and family. The television is kept on for eight hours each day in the average American home—whether or not the average American family is watching it. It may be because of this constant barrage of audio stimuli that, when asked to recall in detail what yesterday's lecture was about, the major point of their boss's weekly update, or even the dialogue of a favorite television or radio program, most people are able to remember only part of what they listened to. This lack of retention demonstrates that while people hear what goes on around them, they may not be attentive listeners and thus are not processing all the information that they are capable of remembering.

Everyone has had the experience of thinking, "If only I could remember what she said," or "I didn't really understand why he said to do this." The value of good listening skills is apparent and necessary in all areas of our lives, particularly in interpersonal relationships and in public speaking.

LISTENING

Whether you're speaking to a group or are a member of an audience, you'll need to master the skill of listening. You'll need to hone your listening abilities so that you can truly understand the questions and concerns of your audience, and so that you can listen to other speakers analytically. Analyzing other speakers assists you not only in finding the main points and truth in messages, but also in deciphering what works and doesn't work in the public-speaking arena. Becoming a better listener enables you to critique other speakers and to select positive aspects of their content and delivery that you may want to replicate. The first step in becoming a better listener is to examine what interferes with the process of listening.

What happens is that people set up barriers between what the speaker is saying and their interpretation of that message. People might fake attention to a speaker (daydreaming instead) or refuse to listen because they think that they, not the speaker, have the correct point of view. Sometimes people spend so much time preparing for what they'll say that they neglect to listen to what someone else has to say. Or perhaps people spend so much time writing down every word of a lecture that they don't understand the big picture. Of course, people might also get so caught up in their prejudices about the way someone looks, dresses, or talks that they don't give that person an opportunity to change. Inevitably, such people stand to lose because they haven't opened themselves up to the opportunity to learn. So, what can you do to ensure that you become a better listener? Study the following list of tips, incorporate these points into important listening situations, and notice the positive results. Although these guidelines relate directly to public speaking, they also apply to all other forms of communication.

Remember that becoming a better listener takes time and patience, but the results are worth it.

Tips for Becoming a Better Listener

1. Establish a reason for listening to a lecture, your weekly work meeting, or the assigned class documentary. People remember more if they know why they are listening to something. Will you score higher on an exam, sell more products, or find out more about your best friend? Remind yourself of the benefits.

2. Listen for useful information during a speech. Don't write down every word. Search for main points and important subpoints. You need to understand the whole picture.

3. Eliminate or ignore possible listening distractions. Sit as close to a speaker as you can. If there are physical distractions, try to eliminate them, or ask the speaker to do so. If you are worrying or are angry about something outside of the immediate situation, try to suspend that internal distraction until after you are finished listening.

4. Concentrate on what the speaker is saying. Expend some energy to accomplish this.

5. Be open to the speaker. Withhold negative judgment about the way someone looks or dresses, giving a speaker the opportunity to speak, and yourself the opportunity to learn something.

6. Listen to the entire message before you make a judgment. Give the speaker a chance to establish main points and discuss evidence. It's always best not to jump to conclusions.

---

7. Provide feedback to the speaker. A nodding head or a confused expression will provide your speaker with useful feedback. When it's appropriate, always ask for clarification. Make sure that you understand the speaker's intended message.

8. Analyze your listening skills. Are there certain situations where you have a difficult time listening? Is there a personal style of delivery that alienates you? Recognizing your listening patterns is the first step toward making improvements. After identifying the problem, take the appropriate steps to rectify the situation.

EVALUATION

One of the best ways to improve your public speaking skills is through evaluation. By evaluating yourself and other speakers, and being evaluated by others, you will become quite clear about what makes a great speaker. You'll be able to incorporate these effective components into your own style, perfecting your skills with each evaluation.

Whenever you are in a position to critique someone, it's important to follow some effective tips for offering criticism. Take a look at the following critiquing tips and incorporate them into your evaluation repertoire.

Tips for Offering Criticism

1. Always balance positive comments with remarks about improvement. Even in self-evaluation, look for the strengths as well as weaknesses in your speech.

2. Focus on the facts. State an area where improvement is needed, supporting your assertion with fact. If you tell a speaker to eliminate nonfluencies, know what kind and where the nonfluencies were used.

3. Be specific in your evaluation. Rather than saying, "Good job," be prepared to address the positive aspects and shortcomings of the speech.

4. Try to give your feedback immediately while the speech is still fresh in everyone's mind.

5. Give feedback about things that the speaker can change.

6. Offer criticism with an open, caring attitude. Acting superior closes the door on an open exchange of ideas.

7. Give the speaker a chance to ask you questions about his or her speech. Know what the speaker's concerns and priorities are.

As a speaker, you'll also need to be open to evaluation. Examine the following tips for receiving criticism and work to incorporate them into your listening skills.

Tips for Receiving Criticism

1. Assume your evaluators have something constructive to say. After all, their criticism will tell you how you came across.

2. Don't be defensive; be open to any evaluation. Treat every comment you receive as a gift. Whatever is said will enable you to understand your speech and the audience better. Ultimately this will improve your public speaking skills.

3. Make sure the person who is evaluating you is aware of your priorities and concerns about your speech.

4. Be certain that you understand the comments you receive. If necessary, ask for additional written or verbal clarification.

In order to prepare for your real speech, ask audience members to fill out forms during or after a rehearsal. The forms should also be completed by some or all of your audience during or after your actual speech. In addition, these evaluation forms are excellent guides when critiquing a videotape of your speech. Maintain an evaluation file and periodically review your forms in order to pinpoint those areas that need improvement. Notice that this book has addressed all of the criteria listed in these evaluation forms.

SPEAKER EVALUATION

Name _____

Specific Purpose _____

Date _____

Title _____

Please write comments for each criterion.

Did the introduction engage the audience and introduce the topic?

_____

Were the main points clear and organized?

_____

Was the conclusion memorable and did it prepare the audience for the end?

_____

Did the speaker maintain eye contact, and was he or she effective with other nonverbal delivery?

_____

Did the speaker use his or her voice appropriately?

_____

Was the topic interesting and stimulating?

_____

Did the speaker complete the speech on time?

_____

Evaluated by:

_____

PUBLIC SPEAKING EVALUATION FORM

Name _____

Title _____

Date _____

Evaluator _____

Please address the following points:

Was the specific purpose appropriate for the audience and the assignment?

_____

Was the organization conducive for the material?

_____

Did the evidence support the main points?

_____

Was the language appropriate for the audience and the occasion?

_____

Did the vocal delivery maintain interest and accentuate the material?

_____

Did nonverbal delivery reinforce important points and augment the speech?

_____

Was the speech worthwhile and challenging?

_____

SPEECH ANALYSIS

Name _____

Specific Purpose _____

Date _____

Critic _____

Note both strengths and weaknesses of the speech.

1. Did the introduction grab your attention and preview the body of the speech?

   _____

2. Were the main points clear and well organized?

   _____

3. Were the main points well supported?

   _____

4. Did the conclusion reinforce the specific purpose?

   _____

5. Did the speech fulfill its specific purpose?

   _____

6. Did the speaker use effective nonverbal delivery?

   _____

7. Did the speaker have an effective verbal delivery?

   _____

8. What were the strengths of the speech?

   _____

9. What were the areas that the speaker may need to improve?

   _____

EVALUATOR FEEDBACK

Name _____

Specific Purpose _____

Date _____

Critic _____

Write constructive criticism for the following criteria:

1. Text
   Appropriate specific purpose
   Interesting material
   Sufficient information

2. Organization
   Introduction
   Body
   Conclusion
   Transitions
   Evidence
   Language

3. Nonverbal Delivery
   Eye contact
   Stance and posture
   Gestures

4. Verbal Delivery
   Volume and rate
   Pitch
   Pronunciation and enunciation
   Nonfluencies

5. Overall Effectiveness
   Worthwhile
   Interesting

PRESENTATION EVALUATION

Name _____

Date _____

Title _____

Speech Objective _____

Record your comments and rate the speaker on a 1- to 5-point scale.

1 Low
2 Fair
3 Satisfactory
4 Very good
5 Excellent

Comments

I.   Content
    Accomplished objective   _____
    Introduction   _____
    Organization   _____
    Supporting material   _____
    Conclusion   _____

II. Delivery
    Nonverbal   _____
    Verbal   _____
    Use of visual aids   _____

III. External factors
    Lighting, seating,   _____
    and noise

IV. Overall effectiveness   _____
    Total   _____

Use the information from the preceding evaluation forms when you evaluate others as well as when you evaluate yourself. After a while, the criteria on these forms will become commonplace for you, and at that point, you'll know that you have internalized the evaluation process.

Throughout your life, you will continue to perfect your speaking ability; however, at certain times, you may feel as if your abilities have hit a plateau. This is perfectly normal because most people develop in spurts, level off for a short while, and then make progress again. The following list of guidelines for public-speaking success may help when things aren't progressing the way you'd like and will keep you honest when things are going exceptionally well.

Guidelines for Public Speaking Success

- Remember that speaking is a lifelong learning process. You're never too good or too old to learn a new technique or understand a new concept. Stay open to learning.

- Speak at every occasion you can. Join a speech club, volunteer to give a talk, and take every opportunity to apply the speaking skills you've learned.

- Critique other speakers whenever you can. By recognizing the strengths and weaknesses of others, you'll know what to integrate into your style.

- Keep an ongoing speech file of articles, speeches, and other materials that will help you write or deliver speeches in the future.

- Seek evaluation from others about your speeches. Be open to criticism. Eliminate defensiveness from your repertoire of responses.

- Always complete a self-evaluation after speaking. To accomplish this, videotape or audiotape your speech. Keep a notebook of your evaluations to identify patterns of behavior. Your records should indicate when and where the speech was given, the specific purpose, the content of the speech, the audience's response, and what you considered your strengths and weaknesses to be.

- Remember that you are responsible for your speeches. It's up to you to prepare, rehearse, and take command when you speak. Occasionally you'll make a mistake (everyone does); the important thing is how you handle it.

- When appropriate, incorporate humor into your speeches. Humor can reduce stress for you and your audience.

SUMMARY

This chapter discussed the importance of listening, barriers that may interfere with listening, and tips for improving your listening skills. The chapter also included ideas for giving and receiving criticism as well as evaluation forms and guidelines for continual progress in public speaking. By incorporating this information and the material from the rest of the book into your skills, you will succeed at mastering the art of public speaking.

Notes

Notes

Notes

Notes

Notes

Notes

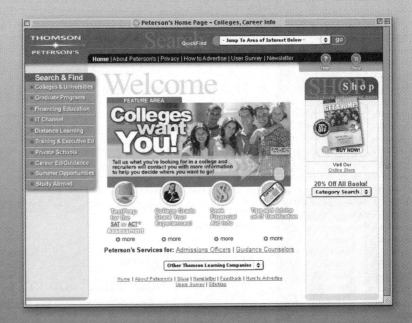